Have Kids, They Said

ALYSIA LOWE EHLE

DEDICATION

Dedicated to my daughter who covered herself in Vaseline while I was editing this book

ACKNOWLEDGMENTS

Thank you to my husband, Kyle, for his endless love and support in everything I choose to do, and his dedication to our marriage and life together as we raise our two beautiful daughters. Thank you to my friends who provided me with inspiration and guidance—not only as contributions to write this book, but to navigate life with children. Thank you to my daughters, who have helped ground me and recognize what is truly important in life.

1 INTRODUCTION

"Have kids!" they said.

"It'll be fun!" they said.

Perhaps I should have prepared myself for what it meant to embark on the journey of parenthood. But, alas—I never read a single baby book.

Correction: I have never read a single book to this day. Even with two kids.

I've read plenty of books about caterpillars and bunnies who play hide and seek to my babies— but I've never read one book about parenting.

When we first had Brooklyn, I admitted this and wondered whether I'd be better off having done more than flip through the free copy of What to Expect While You're Expecting that my doctor gave me. I knew my body was going to change. I knew my life was going to change. Did I really need a book to outline every detail? Isn't parenting something you just figure out?

Well, I am living proof that that is true. We did just figure it out. And we figured out a lot of things that weren't just how to take care of a baby. This may sound unconvincing for you to even continue reading my book. The point, though, isn't about what I didn't read. It's about what I couldn't read because I don't think it exists. Until now.

The real story about motherhood has not yet been written because it's not necessarily a pretty one. It's a story that many women put a filter on when talking to someone who is pregnant. Or someone without kids. Or maybe, they don't even think about their real story of motherhood. Their subconscious is playing tricks on them, creating the facade that having children is just 'so great.' Because their subconscious knows they should try to do it all over again to provide their child a sibling playmate to relieve themselves of being the only non-imaginary attendee to this week's tea party.

Well, I am not that mother. And I will tell you the real story. And give you the real tips to survive it.

We all know that story you hear about motherhood being 'so great' isn't just a facade. We love our kids! We do. We really do. They are great. But sometimes, we say it so much to convince ourselves, so we don't lose our shit. Yes, motherhood is a rewarding adventure, but it is not without moments of intense and excruciating life lessons. Sometimes, that life lesson is breakfast with a toddler.

At the very least, I want you to know what you're truly up against.

When you become a mother, you realize there is an entire world of shit you wish someone would have told you. It's the kind of stuff you'd have expected your closest girlfriend to tell you all about. I mean, you're on her speed dial. As soon as you told her you were pregnant, the reality of what you're about to do to your life should have been unveiled by her.

But women don't do that.

It isn't until your first desperately needed girls' night after having a baby, which might just be a bottle of wine and a frozen pizza at that best friend's house, that you will divulge into the reality of motherhood. You will be deep in the trenches of newborn warfare, thinking your own experience is so dark and lonely and dreary, you must be doing something wrong to have lost so many battles. The daily struggle is real. But that night, you'll find out you are actually not alone. Your best friend went through that war, too. She is still going through it. The more you ask around, the more you realize that the other mothers you know are all in the same boat. So are all the other mothers you haven't asked. Some of them even have it worse.

Eventually, you'll find out all about motherhood. The experiences and emotions that are hidden behind a pretty curtain hung up to hide the mess of what's really going on.

Opening up about my own first experiences in motherhood made me realize this. My first maternity leave was miserably lonely. And upon admitting this to my friend—who already had two children—she voiced her concern, "Alysia! I wish you would have called me. I was like this, too."

But how would I have known that? And why did it seem like declaring my dislike for my new role in life would have been a burden? Or come across as ungrateful? I mean, it was probably the hormones. And also, the shimmering societal outlook of women with children.

Why is it that before you actually have a baby, no one really talks to you about what being a parent is like. Or what being pregnant is really like. That you might think for a couple of seconds you've ruined your life—and that it's okay to have small moments of doubt. It's okay because the next microsecond of thought, you might be floating in a pillow of newborn cuddles and coffee and everything feels perfect. But then that newborn-cuddle high takes a cliff dive, because the next day you scream directly in your newborn's face because you don't know what in the living hell is wrong with her, and you cannot physically stand to suffer through another minute of crying, because it is some horrendous kind of torture probably used in a dark room by the CIA.

That might sound extreme, and I will sheepishly admit I did actually scream in my colicky newborn's face once. I was at my wit's end, which is when I walked outside and repeated my mantra…I love my kids. I do. I really do. They are great.

There are days when you have everything under control. You're killin' this parenting thing. It's Friday, and the baby took two solid naps, ate two extra ounces. You not only washed two loads of laundry—you actually folded and put them away where they belong, instead of letting them sit on the living room couch half-folded, only to actually use them to dress your family before they all go straight back in the hamper. You washed your hair, you put on real clothes and you even cooked your family dinner. You've been a mom for about six weeks and it finally feels like life is coming together again. There just has to be a hint of normalcy around the corner because life cannot simply go on in chaos and stress and fatigue forever. It's just a scientific fact.

I will warn you now. As soon as that picture-perfect day happens, within a couple of days, you will have one of the worst nights of your life with your baby. It may not be the actual worst, but the pitfall is so great it feels like an all-new low. Because that is parenting and that is just scientific fact.

I would know. I'm a scientist.

I'm telling you this because it's what happened to me. And I was so utterly unprepared for all the real situations and the raw emotion. The no-bullshit, actual life things that happen. You can read all the books you want about the tactical methods of raising a baby. Who really writes those books anyway? I'm willing to bet they are not written by someone who has just gone through newborn warfare. You need to read a book written by an ordinary mom. One that tells you about how you're going to feel. Not some fluff about changing your baby's diaper every hour or fluctuating hormones or a cutesy thing called 'baby blues.' You need to understand that you might cry for days and feel inadequate and wonder what happened to your life or if it is ever going to feel normal again.

I'd also encourage that you chat with your friends about motherhood. And if the first opinion you get is only that 'it's the best thing that ever happened,' then you need to find a new friend and get a better review, because they are not all five stars. Although I can't argue against the ideal that children are incredibly amazing and serious blessings from heaven, there's a lot of not-so-heavenly moments that come along with them.

You will cry. You will scream. You will pick your kid's nose. You will pee your pants a little when you sneeze. You might have to wear diapers home from the hospital and rinse your hoo-ha with a water bottle because it hurts too much to use toilet paper.

It's inevitable to feel insufficient at some point. But you're not. It's nearly impossible not to feel alone. But you're not. Even if you're the first of your friends to have a baby and they don't understand, you know someone who has had a baby and you need to find her. Stalk her down on Facebook messenger like you just joined an affiliate marketing company and you need to build your pyramid. And instead of talking to her about some weight-loss shake you just tried, ask if you can talk to her about motherhood. She will know what you're going through and I bet she will listen and meet you for a play date or grab a coffee. She might even be that person with whom you share a bottle of wine and a frozen pizza. Because ultimately, motherhood is a tribe and we're all here to support.

You are not alone! Every mother feels like they lose it at times. No one has it all together. It can look like it from the other side of an Instagram filter, but everyone has their own frustrations.

That's what you need to know, and that's what you need to read before you have a baby. No one actually tells you that your boobs will leak all over the place when your milk comes in or that you'll have uncomfortable pain from getting stitches in your nether region. No one tells you that your life will be a mess. No two experiences are the same, but none of them are really all that different either. You should listen to at least one mother's experience before you have your own. It will help you be better prepared and know that it's normal to feel all your emotions within one day and sometimes feel like you're lost. Lost in your emotions. Or lost in a bag of potato chips. Quite possibly at the same time.

And in all honesty, I have thought that it may be taboo to write this book, simply because it may offend some women. Talking about pregnancy and parenting this way might be construed by some as complaining—especially to those who have struggled for years to conceive. And I can understand that. It's another hard reality that many of us had an easier time making a baby than others. But one woman's tough journey into motherhood doesn't negate how hard it is to raise a child either. I don't think anyone's experience should be denounced in any kind of way. Plus, this book is only meant to shed some light on the dark days of motherhood. It's meant to make you laugh and say 'Oh, this shit is spot on.' Offending people is sometimes just a part of life. I guess if you're offended, you'll just have to deal with it or stop reading.

I am not an expert in pregnancy or parenting—nor am I claiming to be. I am, however, an expert in my own pregnancy experience. I've had two. Brooklyn was born in 2016, and Charlotte was born in 2018. It was after Charlotte was born that I decided women should read a book about a real-life story because I wish that I had. As you read, you'll also find thoughts and recommendations from other women, because more opinions are better than one. This book is sarcastic and uncensored. If you don't like either of these things, then this isn't the parenting book for you. I chose to write this book fresh out of pregnancy with a 'colicky' three-month-old, so I apologize in advance if my opinions seem a bit turbulent. But turbulence is the worst part of any flight and I am here to turn on the seatbelt sign.

Buckle up, ladies. Let's get ready for takeoff into the dark and twisty life of motherhood.

2 GETTING PREGNANT AND GETTING YOUR LIFE TOGETHER

It's most likely not news to you that getting pregnant can be hard. I assume that you've already done it, or you've already been trying. If so, you'll know that it doesn't always happen with the snap of a finger.

Although sometimes it does. And that's awesome for you if it did!

But for many women, it's a long journey. You'd think that getting pregnant would be really easy. It seems easy, right? I mean, how much effort did you put into trying NOT to get pregnant. The pills, the patches, the rings, the IUDs, the condoms, the 'pulling it out.' Removing all these barriers surely means that getting pregnant should be a piece of cake. How else do accidental pregnancies happen anyway? (A real question I have asked myself.)

But once you start trying to have kids, you realize there is a long road ahead. Whether it's planning for the journey or figuring out your obstacles along the way. Before they even exist, you start to picture your life with kids and realize how much your life will change. Or maybe, how much it needs to change. This chapter is called 'getting your life together,' after all.

Most of my life, I wanted nothing to do with children. I didn't have a lot of experience around babies or children besides my siblings. Even then, I was still a child myself. If you'd have asked anyone in my family, they'd tell you there's no way I'd have kids. Even when I first met my husband, I wasn't sure I wanted kids. Whether I actually thought I'd be childless forever is totally up for debate, seeing as how I now have two children of my own. But it felt true at the time, maybe because I didn't want to admit I'd ever want children, or maybe because the thought of having children seemed so scary.

Somewhere between meeting Kyle and accepting his marriage proposal, I realized I would, in fact, want children 'someday.' Maybe it was love that convinced me. (I am not a sap and saying this makes me roll my eyes a little.) Maybe it was my biological clock. Maybe it was the fact that God knew we'd make some seriously beautiful babies. (Everyone's babies are beautiful. But mine? BEAUTIFUL.) But I knew I'd want kids 'someday.'

What is 'someday'? It is far away and fairly noncommittal, so I didn't put too much thought into it. That is until we were drunk one night. We'd only been married a few months. Kyle said he would be ready to have kids at any time, whenever I decided I was ready, too. He confirmed the next morning in a more sober state that his drunk statement was actually true. (As most things are, the truth always comes out with a little booze. It's called liquid courage for a reason.) He knew I wasn't ready yet and said whenever I wanted to pull the trigger, he'd be on board.

What a weird thing it is for your husband to be ready for children before you. Aren't women the ones who want to have kids first? It seems that way, long before you ever have a conversation about it. There was never a point in my life when I had 'baby fever.' I didn't really get it, and even though I knew I wanted kids, I think it was more of an obligation I had to fulfill in life than a true yearning to have a baby of my own.

I say an obligation because I believe my words were literally, 'Let's get it over with.' To me, pregnancy sounded like the worst thing ever. I like to be in control, and I did not want to lose control of my body and my life. I had admitted I wanted children, but pregnancy was not something I wanted to experience.

Besides, there were weddings and parties and concerts that I wanted to attend, and I obviously couldn't be pregnant for any of that! We spent a few months talking about what I should and shouldn't be pregnant for, thinking about when all our single friends and siblings might get married so we could plan our children's birth around these events that may literally never even happen. Finally, Kyle told me I can't plan our life around everyone else's life, especially since getting pregnant isn't always easy. I knew he was right. So, I ripped off the proverbial band-aid.

'Let's get it over with.'

We tried to get pregnant in our first year of marriage. We got married in May 2014 and decided in December to give it a whirl. I had been off birth control for a while, and I used an app to track my ovulation schedule. We tried for about two weeks, then looked at each other and wondered if we were really ready. We had just gotten married. I was soul-searching to figure out what I was going to do with my life after finishing my PhD. We were focusing on paying off a mountain of student loan debt. We worked out several different budget scenarios of what we could afford for baby budgets, daycare, and how much we'd have to save every month to pay for the actual birth of a child.

'We should probably wait until we're in a better financial position.'

Having sex with the intention of getting pregnant is weird and scary. Definitely weird, considering you've spent a large portion of your life having sex and trying not to get pregnant. It's weird, but it's even more scary. You can talk all day long about being ready to have kids, but when you're actually trying to, things start feeling real even though there is no baby yet. We likely buried our fears in financial excuses. We stopped trying.

Two weeks later, I almost fainted from being over-heated in a shopping mall with Kyle's mom and sisters. And then my period was two days late.

I peed on a stick and found out I was pregnant. And I panicked.

I sat on Kyle's lap and ugly cried. We weren't ready. Even though I had previously committed to having children, we called off the whole pregnancy thing. I was not mentally prepared to have a child. And what were we going to do about money? We realized we couldn't actually afford a kid, and yet, here we were, knocked up after our first month of trying.

Kyle was probably just as scared as me, but he was calm and told me it'd be fine. He hugged me as I snotted all over his shirt.

It seemed surreal.

I had no idea how pregnancy calendars worked and was surprised to find out that by the time you take a test, you're technically already four weeks pregnant. I didn't have an OB that I loved, so I sought out some recommendations from my few friends who had babies. While I was surprised to find out I was four weeks pregnant, I was more surprised to find out that a doctor doesn't even see you until you're eight weeks pregnant. That's a whole month between peeing on a stick and getting a sonogram. It seems like an eternity of just waiting around to see if this thing is real or not.

Only four weeks along, I felt just fine. I was working out but cutting out caffeine, lunch meat and soft cheeses. At week five, I started to feel a little queasy in the mornings. I was eating chicken noodle soup for breakfast. And I started getting these horribly awful leg cramps that kept me up all night long.

The cramps lasted about a week, then things settled down a little. My stomach wasn't really as nauseous, and I wondered if I was really going to get morning sickness at all. Some women don't and they are the luckiest.

At the time, I was working as a post-doctoral fellow at UT Southwestern Medical Center. I had done some studies there as part of my PhD and came on as a mentee to a doctor working clinical trials. One morning at work, I ran to the bathroom before heading up to a procedure. And I found brown spotting in my underwear.

I don't remember if I actually went to the procedure or not. I do remember frantically calling Kyle, then calling my doctor's office. The annoying thing about calling a doctor's office is that it's usually required you just leave a message and wait for someone to call you back. My cell phone service sucked in my office space, so I waited by the bathroom window where I'd actually get cell service so I could find out what was going on. Surely some spotting is normal in pregnancy, and they'd tell me to relax and lay down. It would all be just fine.

While they did tell me that some spotting is normal, they advised I either drive up to their office or go to the Emergency Room to make sure things were checking out okay. I decided to go to the ER. After all, I was already at a hospital.

So, I called Kyle and he came down to meet me at the Parkland Emergency Room for what would eventually be one of the worst days of my life.

I haven't told you this yet, but I'm afraid of needles. Severely. When I finally got called back to see a doctor, they started with a blood draw. Somehow, that was the smoothest part of the day. I'd already waited an hour. After reviewing my medical history and discussing why I was there in the first place, they sent me down to the Parkland Women's Clinic.

If you are not from Dallas, or not familiar with Parkland, it's a hospital dedicated to helping the 'indigent and needy.' Not to sound crass, but you never know who you're going to find there because it's usually a lot of homeless people. It's wonderful that Dallas has a great hospital dedicated to helping the needy, but the better decision for me that day would have been to turn around and drive the hour it would take to get to my doctor's office. There were some rough-looking women in that clinic. Many of them probably should not have been pregnant. One pregnant woman left the waiting room, saying she needed a cigarette.

We sat in the waiting room for six hours. Parkland was in the process of building a beautiful new hospital, but the clinic was in the old building. It was dark and dirty. I remember being starving, not having eaten all day. There was a giant 'no food or drink' sign on the door, yet several people had brought in bags of McDonald's. Waiting rooms are never comfortable, to begin with, and I was scared about what would happen. It was agonizing.

When I finally got called back, they asked Kyle to stay in the waiting room. They reviewed medical history again. They also had to do more blood work. The room I was in was freezing and the doctor I had wasn't much warmer. They ran some more tests and noticed that my blood sugar was really low, likely because I had waited to get called back so long causing me not to eat all day. They gave me some juice, then sent me over for a sonogram.

The technician who performed the sonogram was much friendlier than the doctor, but this room was even colder than the one before. I was wearing my hospital scrubs and a light jacket that didn't provide much warmth. I was shivering so badly, not only from the temperature but also from fear of my first vaginal sonogram revealing the truth I already knew. He had a hard time even reading the sonogram because I was shaking so much. They had to bring in some blankets and wait for me to get warm enough to keep still for a few minutes, so he could see what was going on.

After the sonogram, they called Kyle back to my room. My bloodwork showed that my hCG levels were very low for being 6 weeks along. It meant I was most likely not pregnant. They couldn't find a heartbeat on the sonogram, but that is not unusual since it was so early. I was advised to go see my doctor the next day if the bleeding continued. We were ready to go home, but they wouldn't let me leave because my blood sugar was still so low. They gave me crackers and more juice, and we waited another hour after what had already been the longest day of my life.

I went to the ER at 1 pm, and we left the women's clinic after 10 pm. We were exhausted. I walked with Kyle to his truck, and he drove me to my car. He gave me a big hug and then we parted ways—me driving towards home and Kyle towards Taco Bell.

When I got home, all I wanted to do was shower, eat my CrunchWrap Supreme, and crawl in bed. I turned on the water and waited for it to get warm, but after 10 minutes, it was ice cold. Kyle was finally home, and I threw on my robe to tell him what was going on. He went to check the water heater and found that its closet, along with the back bedroom and bathroom, was flooded. Talk about a great way to end a not-so-stellar day.

I took a cold shower, ate my food and crawled in bed. The next morning, I woke up to the worst cramps of my life and a full-fledge period. I was indeed having a miscarriage.

I ended up driving to my doctor alone because the flooding from the day before was caused by a burst pipe underneath our house. The only doctor's appointment I could get was the same time we had a plumber scheduled to come and dig out underneath our house. Kyle felt awful about it, but there wasn't much we could do. I had to sit through another vaginal sonogram and another technician tell me they weren't seeing anything.

I never ended up seeing this doctor again, but she was incredibly sweet. She told me what I had experienced was a chemical pregnancy. In a chemical pregnancy, an egg gets fertilized and implants itself in the uterus. hCG is produced, and this is what triggers a positive pregnancy test. But for unknown reasons, the egg never full implants itself, causing the pregnancy to fail after a week or two. She said that although it's very emotionally troubling, the good news is that it means my body can get pregnant, and it can sometimes 'rev up' the system for when you're ready to try again.

It was an emotional shit storm. I went from bawling my eyes out for getting pregnant in the first place, to incredible pain. Physical pain from the miscarriage cramps, and emotional pain from just losing what I thought was a baby inside me. A baby I wasn't even sure I was ready for in the first place.

Later that day, we acknowledged our feelings but also that we felt it was a sign from God. After a day like we'd had, coming home to a couple thousand dollars' worth of damage to your home could only be a sign that you're not ready just yet. It was God's way of showing me I did want children, but that this was just not the right time for it.

We waited five months to start trying again, shortly after our first wedding anniversary. Four months later, I got a positive pregnancy test. I was elated, feeling emotionally ready and knowing that a baby was part of our life plan.

After my own experience, I decided I would never again ask a woman when she will have kids if I didn't know her well, or we'd never discussed the topic before. You don't know where anyone is in their journey, and that a question as simple as 'Have you decided when you will have kids?' could be extremely painful. It's such a simple gateway for conversation and a common topic for small talk, but there's plenty of other unassuming things to talk about. Like the weather.

I share my experiences with the hopes that it might help you feel at peace with timing for your own pregnancy. I truly believe that 'God's plan' has its own obstacles and a timeline that probably doesn't match what you desire. In the grand scheme of things, I do know that our own obstacles to getting pregnant were far less enduring than that of other families.

I know a woman who had multiple miscarriages before conceiving a son after years of trying.

And a woman who tried for years to have a second baby only to have twins after getting divorced.

One of my best friends can't physically have kids naturally, so IVF is the only option she and her husband have to conceive.

I know several women who had babies after 36-year-old in what doctors lovingly refer to as a 'geriatric pregnancy.'

And I know a woman who carried her baby for 8 months, only to discover her child's heart had stopped beating in the womb.

Getting pregnant is scary and emotional. Even though I may have been 'ready,' no one is actually ready. There is no way to fully prepare yourself for such a life-changing event. The best thing we can do is trust that our journey is taking us somewhere for a reason, and that might mean children aren't in the picture when you want them, or how you expect to get them.

Although physically having a child is a life-changing event, I'd like to argue that even trying to have kids is life-changing as well. There are also some things that prevent women from getting pregnant. Things that are completely out of their control. But some women need to change the way they eat or exercise in order to have children, and some women undergo many procedures to even have a chance.

I didn't have a period at all for a long time. It was in my late teens/early twenties. I never knew if it was from the birth control I was on, or if it was from treating my body so poorly for a really long time. When I was in high school, I had a serious disorder with eating. I was anorexic, but it was paired with binge eating and binge drinking. I remember days where I'd skip all my meals so I could eat ice cream for dinner, or days when I could not allow myself to eat more than 600 calories. And when the weekend came, I'd drink my face off and eat everything in sight. The weekends were followed with extreme bouts of guilt and self-hate, which only fueled me to stop eating and keep that vicious cycle going. I never felt good enough or pretty enough and believed that being skinny was the answer.

Somewhere in my mid-twenties, when I settled into the relationship with my husband, I realized I needed to turn things around. I wasn't as restricting at that time in my life, but I was counting calories and working out a lot. I could just never keep up with what I thought I should look like, and it took a big mental toll on me. It wasn't sustainable. By the time we got married, I gave up counting calories altogether and focused more on just being healthy. I often wonder if I would have been able to get pregnant if I hadn't changed my mindset on my health and myself.

You might not need to change the way you live your life at all. But there is a mental shift you have to make that gets you ready for the ultimate responsibility of raising a child. (And if you think that getting a pet qualifies as an event that gets you ready for raising a child, please do not ever say that to a friend who is pregnant or has a baby. Ever.)

Getting ready for a child means you need to be ready to dramatically change your life. You need to be ready to give up your freedoms. No more spontaneous dinners with friends after work. Sleeping in is a pleasure of the past. You'll probably have to cut down on your Starbucks coffee habit to save money—or whatever your equivalent habit is. Maybe it's shopping? Maybe it's getting your nails done. Basically, you need to really get your life together.

Dramatic change is obvious. You're going to be raising a child! That's another human being that you (and your husband or partner) are solely responsible for nurturing. For making sure that your tiny little human is happy and healthy, both mentally and physically. While you're thinking about the change that will happen in your day-to-day life, you might also want to think about how you're going to actually raise this child. I don't just mean decisions like breastmilk, formula or whether they will sleep in the bassinet or the crib. Even though you'll have some time to decide how you and your partner want to raise your child, it's never too early to start a conversation about the future you want for your family, the example you want to set and the values you want them to inherit.

This is a book about parenting. Parenting does not start and end with birthing a child and the tactical day-to-day decisions you must make. Being a good parent is more about the example you set and casting your values to your children. It is less about cute outfits, or how big the baby shower was or a Pinterest-worthy nursery. Many couples receive pre-marital counseling from their church before they tie the knot. It is less counseling and more thinking about togetherness and what your future life will be like. I think pre-natal counseling should exist as well. I don't know where you'd get it. Maybe a real therapist. But having kids is arguably much more life-altering than getting married. Lots of people get divorced. Children are permanent.

The list of things you can think about is nearly endless and gets longer the more time you spend as a parent. These are some ideas to get a conversation started. You might be surprised how different your views are from your husband on some topics. We definitely were.

Where should you live? Do you plan on relocating closer to family? Farther from family?
How are your school districts? Would you need to enroll your children in a private school? Is that something you'd want to do?
Will you plan to save for your child's college or wedding?
Will your kids get an allowance for doing chores, or will they be expected to help around the house?
Will your kids have to get a job?
What kind of financial guidance will you be providing for them?
Will you teach them the importance of giving?
Will you enroll them in sports against their will?
What kind of life do you want for your child?

On a more serious note—do you know that the things you say and do will influence what your children say and do?

I don't just mean cutting out curse words. Unless you want your children to repeat you, then, by all means, keep them in the vocabulary. (It happened to me. And be sure not to follow your 'dammit' with 'shit' when you realize what you did. Silly Mommy.)

It's not too early to start thinking about your own habits, how you treat others and how you treat yourself.

Let's talk habits. I am going to tell you this short story that makes me cringe every time I think about it. I was sitting at home, playing with newborn Charlotte, and toddler Brooklyn found my cell phone. Unprompted, she ran it up to me and stuck it in my face, 'Here mommy! Here is your phone!' So happy with herself that she helped Mommy stay forever connected to the internet. At the impressionable age of two, she clearly learned that Mommy is always on her phone, so she must have it at all times. It makes me feel disgusted with myself. Scrolling through Instagram is not a priority, but it's a habit that's been formed which often takes the place of my true priorities. That is a habit I've been working to change, so that I may be able to raise my children without the crutch of technology.

Ultimately, the phone will be an easy habit to fix. Netflix, though. That's a different story. Children's movies on demand are sometimes your only key to silence. Don't forget to bookmark this crucial piece of information.

Treating others isn't something I believe I need to cover. Unless you're a complete asshole, I have no doubt you need much instruction on helping your children treat others well. And if you are an asshole, then I probably can't help you, because I don't really like to deal with assholes.

Most importantly, though, I want you to think about how you treat yourself. Are you healthy? Do you take care of your body? How do you talk to yourself? These are important questions we need to ask.

If I ever won the lottery, I would quit my job and go back to school for a second PhD in psychology, so that I could psychoanalyze my life from a professional point of view. For now, you get my non-professional opinions fueled by self-help books and lifestyle podcasts. I've thought a lot about the reasons why I was ever really afraid to have kids, and specifically daughters. I was legitimately terrified when we found out we'd be having a daughter and not a son our first time around. I think that I was so afraid of being a mother for so long because of the relationship I have with my mother. It's better described as a lack of relationship. I wouldn't say that it is necessarily 'bad,' it just really isn't there. It's different for my sisters, but my mother and I have never been on the same page about anything. Because of that, I didn't feel like I knew what it took to be a mother to a daughter. How do you just know the right things to do? How do I know I am doing the right things and not the wrong things? How do I make sure that my relationship with my daughter is solid?

There are two specific things that stand out to me about being raised by my mother. The first is that she never really talked about anything she was feeling. Not to me, at least. Life was certainly not peachy-keen for us. There were financial struggles and my dad had addiction problems (though we're not going into that here). Mom had a tendency to bottle up her emotions and hide away, which in retrospect was a good lesson on how not to communicate. I saw this in my parents' marriage. Issues weren't raised until they were already a problem, which usually just resulted in drunken tears.

As it turned out, I ended up doing the exact same thing, having observed my parents' marriage for years on end. Early in my relationship with Kyle, there were a lot of silly drunken tears. And a lot of big fights because of it. I'd get mad, then get hammered and unleash the beast. This was a critical point of development for me in my relationship with Kyle. While he also had his own communication skills to work on, mine were basically non-existent. Communication is important, and I had to work on being comfortable talking about how I felt instead of burying it away deep inside and letting it explode at a later date.

The second thing is negativity. It almost doesn't make sense because my mom will often preach how positive thinking can change your life. Whether that outlook was the result of a turning point in her own life after my parents got divorced, I don't know because I can't pin it down. It seems a bit ironic that she has always been a 'free spirit' but in my adolescence, I managed to come away with an underlying sense of negativity that rooted itself in complaining. She always needed to lose weight. She never had any good clothes to wear. Nothing was ever as good as it should be. The house was never good enough or clean enough. She didn't have the job she wanted. Never enough. Not enough.

And sometimes, the negativity was rooted in thoughtlessness. I have a memory of being at my parents' pool the summer after I graduated high school. I was in the beginning of my eating disorder. (My dad was the one who tried to have a conversation with me about it, which I furiously denied. I was holding a piece of string cheese when he confronted me. I unwrapped it and waved it around like a wand that cures eating disorders, then I ate it to prove that he was false. The issue was dropped and never spoke of again, left for me to deal with and eventually cure on my own.) That day at the pool she was talking with one of my sisters about cellulite. My sister must have been complaining about it. I don't remember the exact way it happened, but I vividly remember that she pointed at me and said, "See! Even Alysia has cellulite." I was astonished that she would point out one of my flaws like that. Especially considering how I was clearly sensitive when it came to my own body image.

I never, ever want my daughters to feel down about themselves because of something I said or did, even if it was meant to make her sister feel better.

Words have power. I was very negative for the longest time. When you grow up surrounded by men and women who talk negatively about themselves, you are bound to do the same thing. Children are impressionable and live by example. In a world with so much scrutiny about body image, and creating a social media perfect life, it is more important than ever to provide them with positivity. Show them that they are enough, which starts by knowing that you are enough.

I don't mean to cast blame on my mother. She was dealing with a lot of her own issues, which is obvious because they did get divorced. I also don't know whether my attitude in life would have been different without this negative influence. The world is full of negativity and materialism. I'd have been exposed in some way. But it can only help to provide more positivity than negativity. I would also say that our relationship is better now than it was 10 years ago, though I'll admit neither of us has worked on it as much as we should.

I made a vow to myself to never speak negatively about my body, my achievements or our life in front of my children. Fat is the new f-word. If you fail, don't beat yourself up. Think about the situation and learn from it. I never want my daughters to grow up and think it's acceptable to treat themselves poorly, so I need to take that as advice for myself.

Negativity is not a mindset that is easily changed, but I think it's important to be aware of how you're portraying your words and yourself. Raising kids isn't easy. It's constant work to be the role model you want them to have. But what really is a role model as a parent, anyway?

It is not based on material things, or your looks, or how fancy your job title sounds. It is based on your values. My values include my family, health and creativity. I want to be a parent who provides love, encouragement and support whether it's my child's first steps across the living room or across a stage at graduation. I want to provide them comfort, knowing that what we have and who we are is enough.

Is this a complete digression from the conversation we started with? Perhaps. But there is no better time to evaluate your values than when you get ready to have kids and envision a life with children. It's the first step to getting your life ready to welcome them.

I have no doubt you'll do amazing. Some days will be better than others because that is just life. Nobody is perfect. And on the days that you aren't so amazing, don't be hard on yourself. We all accidentally drop the 'f word' a time or two. (Just me? Okay.)

All you can do is think about the life you want your kids to have and do your best to provide that for them. That can often mean a change in your attitude and behavior that will serve you well to start before you know when they'll arrive.

I mentioned earlier that throughout the book you'll find thoughts, opinions and recommendations from other women and parents. As a forever student, I am always curious to learn anything from other people. No two marriages, parents, children or experiences are the same. I like to glean a little bit of knowledge from a lot of different places to make it work for my own life. I suggest you do the same!

What is the most important advice you would give to new parents?

- Keep open and constant communication with your partner in your parenthood journey. Whether it is before, during or after you've had a baby, if you are feelin' the feels, let it out. Don't bottle it in. Talking things through may help you feel better!
- It goes by too fast! Enjoy every moment you have with them.
- Buy gas drops, a baby carrier with back support and good eye cream. Also, know that it is okay to say 'no' to plans and unsolicited advice that is sure to come!
- Things change literally every day, so don't get too comfortable!
- Sleep whenever you can.

3 BEING PREGNANT

Last chapter we were getting pregnant. That chapter was much more serious and philosophical than I excepted. Maybe even a little inspiring and helpful? I hope.

Last chapter we were encouraged. We were happy and celebrating sticks filled with our urine.

This chapter we're pregnant. And we might be scared or miserable. Or scared and miserable.

I believe the general expectation of pregnancy is that women should love it. Women should have that beautiful glow full of love and affection for the little baby growing in the womb. We should stand around in cute, bump-fitting maternity clothes, resting our hands on our bellies as our maternal instincts are already there to protect the baby from harm. We're expected to be more excited than tired. To not miss drinking alcohol. To not complain about pregnancy because it is a blessing.

Some women have pregnancies like this. It isn't until you join the club that you realize most women don't.

<u>The Unknown</u>

Let's get over my already apparent distaste for pregnancy and admit that when you first get pregnant, it can be really exciting. I was even excited my second time around after I had experienced the horror once before. This life event you've been mentally preparing for is finally here! Congrats! Time to celebrate and pop champagne.

I mean…your husband can pop champagne. You are going to need to spend the next 9 weeks casually (or awkwardly) avoiding your friends, family and social gathering so that no one picks up on the fact that you're knocked up. Maybe that makes me sound like a bit of a lush but turning down alcohol was a sure sign from my friends and family that there was something going on. I mastered the 'fake drinking' pretty well with my pregnancies—either a mixed drink with water or swapping drinks with your husband every now and then so it looks like you're finishing a drink. (Lucky for him, he'll have a built-in designated driver for quite some time.)

So, why are you dodging your friends for the next 9 weeks? Your doctor will likely advise you to be cautious about who you decide to tell until you make it through the first trimester. This is because there is a lot of scary, unknown things that can happen until you make it through those first 13 weeks. Some estimates show that 25% of all pregnancies end in miscarriage. This is also something you don't realize until you get pregnant—that miscarriages are very common, and you probably know a few families that have experienced them.

That fact can sometimes make your first trimester scary, and a little lonely. Especially if you are experiencing a pregnancy after miscarriage. You may be less inclined to tell your friends or family for fear of it happening again, worrying until you hit that 13 weeks and feel in the clear. It's a delicate time, and if you're experiencing some horrific pregnancy symptoms, you may feel even worse. Although my doctor did tell me that being severely nauseous was a 'good sign,' nothing is guaranteed. He may have said that to make me feel better. Nothing you do can prevent a miscarriage from happening, and that is the scariest part. Everyone is comfortable telling their news at different stages in their pregnancy. We waited until we were almost through the first trimester with Brooklyn since we previously experienced a miscarriage that no one really knew about.

A lot of you will probably end up telling at least someone who understands what you're going through. Your husband can be a great sounding board for your feelings and fears, but he cannot sympathize with you because he will never experience the horror that can be like the first trimester.

The Nausea

I had serious envy for women who felt fantastic throughout their pregnancies. Some women don't get morning sickness at all, and it boggles my mind how pregnancy can affect every woman so differently. The cruel truth about 'morning sickness' is that it is certainly NOT designated for just the morning. With Brooklyn, it hit me around 6 weeks, and it hit HARD. One morning I felt fine, and the next I felt like I caught the flu that turned into what felt like a never-ending plague. Food doesn't sound good, and the nausea can make it hard to sleep at night. I ran a healthy recipe blog at the time, and I had to quit because even looking at a picture with vegetables on Instagram made me want to vomit. The weird thing is that I never actually did puke. I definitely tried in hopes it would make me feel better, but nothing really took the nausea away.

Work was a real struggle for me until about 8 weeks when I finally told my boss I was pregnant. We heard a heartbeat at our first sonogram, so we felt it might be okay. I didn't want to tell her so early, but I had worried it would look bad that I used a few sick days, worked from home a few days and left promptly at 5 pm on the days I was in office. I was commuting to work by train to avoid paid parking in downtown Dallas, and it was incredibly miserable.

As I expected, she was incredibly supportive and understanding, providing flexibility until I was feeling myself again. And I also learned that for all three of her pregnancies, she experienced hyperemesis gravidarum, which is nausea so severe it caused dehydration and required hospitalization. In that moment, I felt incredibly grateful to have a work environment that would provide me with that flexibility, but also that my situation was not worse than it was.

Until 11 weeks, I continued to have my colleagues avoid sitting next to me in conference rooms for fear they might catch my 'plague.' I was often cast a sideward glance as I ate Ramen noodles for lunch three days in a row in place of the typical supremely healthy meal of kale salads. After my announcement, it all made sense and my frequent trips to the bathroom and overall dismal-looking state weren't so surprising anymore.

If you experience morning sickness so bad that it interferes with your daily life, you can talk to your doctor about options to help alleviate it. Personally, I got on a prescription that helped to alleviate nausea. It didn't take it away completely but certainly dulled it. One of my friends had it so badly that she required a port in her arm for medicine delivered by an IV. Some women also drink ginger tea or wear balance bracelets used for seasickness to help. Whatever your case, I hope that you can work with your doctor to find something that will get you through it!

<u>The Body Changes</u>

Earlier in this chapter, I described a picture of a woman with that beautiful pregnancy 'glow.' I don't know where the term 'pregnancy glow' came from because I have not personally seen it exist in any pregnant women I know. Except for when it was over 100 degrees and while 8 months pregnant, I walked outside to check the mail. But that wasn't a glow, I was just glistening with sweat.

Seriously though, being big and pregnant in the middle of the summer is no joke. Charlotte was due on September 8, 2018. Every time I announced it, at least one woman would say, "Aw, that means you'll be pregnant during the summer." Per usual in my annoyance for people who state the obvious, I rolled my eyes as they turned away because, yea, I'd be pregnant in the summer. I would think, "So, it might be kinda hot. I've dealt with Texas summer before!"

It wasn't until our first week of 100-degree weather that I realized those women just felt badly for me because summer pregnancies are straight-up awful. I couldn't escape the heat even from inside my house. I carried a fan around to every room I sat in so I wouldn't feel like I'd pass out from heat exhaustion. I felt sweaty and gross at all times, even as I sat next to my husband on the couch, who required a blanket because our A/C was turned down to 68 degrees just to make me feel half-way comfortable. I spent hardly any time outside. Sitting in a pool was too hot and uncomfortable. Not only was I hot, but my belly prevented me from moving freely and I felt trapped inside my own body for months.

Although I didn't experience it in my first pregnancy, the heat brought along swelling in my hands and my feet. Some women have this even in cooler weather. I wasn't able to wear my wedding rings for about two weeks. Most of my sandals were uncomfortable to wear for long stretches at a time, which was actually okay since I worked from home and was basically house bound for fear of melting away in the scorching outdoor temps. I've seen women with swelling so bad they can't even wear shoes at all! It makes sense, with the amount of extra fluids and blood in your body. But making sense doesn't make it any better.

Speaking of swelling, let's switch to clothes for a minute. Your body is going to change drastically, and obviously, that will require different clothes to wear. Once you have a decent-sized bump, you will come to realize that most maternity jeans are pieces of clothing from hell. Let's back-up, though, because you will probably start wearing maternity jeans even before you start showing. Why? Because you're going to be really, really bloated.

I started wearing maternity jeans or only high-waisted leggings once I hit 7 or 8 weeks. All of the hormones raging in your body can cause some weird issues in your digestive tract and make you feel bloated and gassy. Really sexy symptoms to go along with your fake pregnancy glow. I can say that elastic-waisted maternity jeans might serve you well both before your bump and after pregnancy. But there is a point where those are no longer comfortable because they start to hit in the wrong places and cut into your belly. That's when you'll have some decisions to make. You could wear the jeans that have a large elastic band that pulls all the way over your belly. The problem with these is two-fold. They fall down constantly, requiring you to adjust your pants every time you walk because belts are not a thing when you're pregnant. Most maternity jeans also do not have pockets, which is so counter-intuitive it might drive you crazy as you keep trying to put your Chapstick in a place that doesn't exist. Your other option? You just don't wear any clothing at all.

Kidding! Kind of. There are some other options. The only thing I found comfortable to wear during my summer pregnancy were dresses, but even dresses will stick to you and make you sweaty in all the wrong places. Bump sweat is a thing and it's really disgusting. But who wants to wear a dress every single day, anyways? Or make it worse and rotate the same 4 dresses every single week. Not even enough to get you through all the days of the week, because if you're like me, you'll refuse to invest tons of money in clothing that will only fit you for half a year's time.

Your bump, however, is not the only body change that forces you into new clothes. Your boobs are going to get big, and by big, I mean they could become massive. Your bra and shirt size will change, possibly after you're pregnant as well. Breast sensitivity is also likely to happen, and although it was never unbearable for me, it certainly can be for some women. Again, dresses are a great solution for this problem, because they can be stretchy and non-restricting.

You will miss wearing every single outfit in your closet because maternity clothes are annoying. Even though you'll miss wearing normal clothes, I strongly caution you not to give into shopping urges for anything except shoes and accessories. You might end up with a bunch of cheap crap that doesn't fit you after baby. Take that advice from an experienced pregnant shopper. I desperately missed wearing jeans with a cute t-shirt French tucked in the front, along with my strappy wedge sandals. I mean, that's weirdly specific, but all those items are things you probably can't wear during pregnancy. I did buy a few things that I thought I could transition from early maternity to post-pregnancy, and it just didn't work. I wore them maybe once and then donated. Talk about a waste.

I can picture wearing that French-tucked outfit with a full face of perfectly done makeup and my hair bouncing around in wavy curls as I walk through a room. (Ideally, a bar, since I am not pregnant in this picture, but we'll settle for any general room.) But guess what? Perfect hair and skin are two things that are probably not going to exist for you either.

Yes, it's true that your hair will get thicker during pregnancy. I think it's because your body is in over-production mode growing your child and whatever, but your hair stops falling out and might grow faster. It sounds totally awesome at first. Until the baby inside you starts sucking all the nutrients your body has to offer, leaving your hair dry, brittle and riddled with split ends. I don't remember feeling like the life was sucked out of my appearance with Brooklyn, but Charlotte definitely took any kind of water that could have existed in my hair and my skin.

I legitimately looked like a reptile shedding its outer layer in the first trimester of my second pregnancy. The skin on my arms and legs were dry and flaky, but also my face. No amount of lotion could smooth out my face. I often wear a hefty coat of foundation on my face because I have acne rosacea. But during pregnancy, not only did my face flake off, but both the acne and the rosacea flared up for the first six months. As a result, the foundation looked flaky, and my acne showed through, and I was desperately self-conscious a majority of the time.

So, yea. That whole 'pregnancy glow' thing? Not always the case and it often couldn't be further from the truth.

Not only may your skin flake off, but you'll experience some itching and stretching. As my belly grew, it would itch like crazy. It makes sense, I guess, as the skin grows it becomes uncomfortable. Lotion did help this situation, luckily, and I'd often apply it in the morning and at night, so I didn't look like a fool rubbing my belly raw all day.

As your skin stretches, you might also experience some stretch marks. Stretch marks are hereditary in many cases. I was fortunate enough not to get them anywhere on my body as a result of pregnancy, but it's common to get them on your belly, thighs and chest. You know, all the places you're going to gain weight when you're pregnant. Stretch marks seem to be one of the most feared body changes a pregnant woman can experience, with many women desperate to find a way to make them go away or even prevent them from happening in the first place. Though Google will populate many homeopathic remedies for you, I don't know that any one thing works for all women and in many cases, I'd assume it's not likely to prevent them at all, considering they are typically a result of your genetic make-up.

Stretch marks might be feared by women, but the one thing we all talk about most with pregnancy is the weight gain struggles. It's a total mindfuck. Many of us have spent the majority of our lives trying to lose weight and get in shape—whether that be by exercise, eating healthy or taking on extreme dieting. Pregnancy is nine months of those things not mattering because most of the time, you can't even do it.

Let me break that down.

Yes, you can work out when you're pregnant. Technically. But honestly, it is miserable for a lot of women. The most I could do after about 25 weeks in either pregnancy was walk. Any kind of lower body strength exercise would give me knee pain. Walking up one flight upstairs had me out of breath. For someone who was regularly active in a non-pregnant scenario, this seemed ridiculous. It drove me crazy! Exercise is one of my biggest forms of stress relief, and not having that as an outlet made my body feel worse.

There also may not be good times to work out when pregnant. Sometimes, the only way to work out is early in the morning or late at night. But when you're pregnant, you're also tired, and you might not be able to sacrifice sleep for exercise. I tried this for a while during my first pregnancy and had to give it up. A 5 am workout was doable, but by 9 am I was miserably tired, wanting to fall asleep under my desk at the office. I'm an advocate of exercising for health, but I had to recognize it just wasn't in the picture for me.

What's next? Eating healthily. Yes, you can eat healthy while you're pregnant. Since I am an advocate for all things health, I feel I should chat about nutrition just a quick little moment (from a non-medical advice perspective). Eating healthy, if you can, is extremely important. Not only is it healthy for the baby, but it is healthy for you and can help prevent complications for both you and your child throughout pregnancy and after birth. The kicker though? A lot of women can't physically eat healthy because their stomach can't handle it. Remember my aversion to pictures of vegetables? Carbs are gold and a lot of the time it's more important to just feed your body something it can handle, pop your vitamins and live your life because you cannot let yourself starve. My second pregnancy was significantly healthier for two reasons: less nausea and I had given up dairy in my everyday diet. No dairy meant no pizza, grilled cheese, mac 'n cheese or ice cream, which were basically my four food groups when I was pregnant with Brooklyn. If you are able to eat healthy, you can still gain an appropriate amount of weight during your pregnancy, and your doctor can advise to however much weight that should be. And with healthy eating, you are likely better off on the back end. I mean that both literally and figuratively. I dropped back to my pre-pregnancy weight in four months after having Charlotte, when it took me closer to fourteen after Brooklyn. But if you can't eat healthy because vegetables make you wanna vom, then just eat the next best thing that your stomach can handle and move on. Your weight gain and weight loss experience will be different from mine, and different from your best friend's.

Lastly, we have extreme dieting. That is obviously not going to work when you're pregnant. Regular dieting won't work either. Why? Because you're supposed to eat MORE when you're pregnant. Do you know what you're not supposed to do when you're pregnant? OBSESS about how many calories you're eating. If you are a calorie-tracker, I would highly suggest you stop while pregnant. There are certain guidelines that medical professionals will recommend regarding how much to eat when you're pregnant, such as a certain number of additional calories you should intake per trimester. The reality is you're probably just going to be hungry. Maybe all the time. Just focus on eating mostly healthy foods, and you will be just fine! Don't starve yourself because you think you've already hit your calorie allotment for the day.

Easier said than done though, right? Even with a mostly healthy diet, the pregnancy weight gain was hard for me. It's unsettling to look in the mirror and see your once-slender legs filling out, a belly falling over your pants and a butt crack falling out of your underwear. Oh, and the side boob. The extra side boob that is basically another whole boob under both your armpits. The important thing to remember is that, like most of the troubling stages in pregnancy and parenting, it is temporary. YES, temporary. (Although my side boob is seemingly the last to go.) You will not hold on to that extra weight forever if you really don't want to. Remember it will take time for it to fall off. And unless you're one of the lucky ones, it will not just fall off, but it will take work to eat a little healthier and move a little more. But you will be able to do it when you decide that you are ready. Losing baby weight right away isn't always a priority for moms. Sometimes women find that changing eating habits or exercise habits could impact milk supply. And most doctors don't even clear you to work out until 4 to 6 weeks post-partum. If you're concerned with your weight, these are all things you can talk to your doctor about to find the right approach for you and your baby.

During my pregnancy, Kyle was constantly reminding me that the weight gain is normal and that it's necessary in order to grow a healthy baby. I knew that, but I did have to constantly remind myself. And again, after having our babies, I had to remind myself about weight loss. I'd glance in the mirror and catch a look of disdain on my face. He would remind me that it will take time to lose. As everyone says, 'It took 9 months to put the weight on, and it will require time to take the weight off." I knew that, too, but it wasn't any easier. The losing was harder for me to deal with than the gaining. When you're gaining weight, you have a baby inside you, and the additional weight is easier to justify. While Kyle helped me keep my weight situation in the right frame of mine, he also reminded me many times after our second baby that I'd never have to do it again. We were done with babies! No more of the crazy human-growing hormonal weight gain. Honestly, that helped more than anything.

It might take time to be comfortable in your own skin if you can't shed the weight, stretch marks, acne, or dry hair. But just remember that every woman has body changes that might make her uncomfortable after having a baby. Even women that look like they shrunk right back to their pre-pregnancy bodies after pregnancy. I guarantee you, many of the women who appear to be back to normal don't feel that way. There are ways to make yourself look like you bounced back, using clothes that fit in just the right way to hide all the changes to your body.

In today's society, there is a lot of awareness for us to all be body positive and happy with ourselves and our bodies. I agree that we shouldn't be hard on ourselves because of how our bodies have changed. But I don't think it's right to ignore the fact that we are going to have these feelings at some point, and you're not in the wrong for feeling that way! I don't think there is harm in acknowledging that your body has changed and that we want to be comfortable with our bodies again. I also think it is possible to be positive but want to elicit change. Getting back into a healthy routine after a baby is naturally going to mean weight loss—there is just some time and patience that comes along with it.

The Aches and Pains

Pregnancy can be painful.

We could just end this part of the chapter here because anything I tell you right now might be completely different from what you're going to experience. For some reason, an actual pregnancy itself is not synonymous with pain. Labor is certainly associated with pain, although I can honestly say that my labor experience was less painful than my pregnancy experience. (Recovery, though, was more brutal.) Labor was less painful mostly because it's much shorter, you can get an epidural and it's a means to an end. Pregnancy was 9 months of various discomfort, whether it was in my digestive, muscular or nervous system. (Bringing you back to fifth-grade biology with that one.)

If you really think about what happens to your body when you grow a baby, pain almost needs to be a part of it. There is no way your body can expand, double its amount of fluid, gain fat, and shift around all your organs without any discomfort. When you grow a baby, it doesn't just extend out as part of your body. Everything inside you is impacted in some way. After I gave birth to Charlotte, I could literally FEEL my organs sliding back into a place they belong. It's a weird sensation to describe and even weirder to experience.

A lot of the pain women experience is pressure or muscle soreness from the growing bump. Sciatic pain is common, which can be pain in the lower back or legs from pressure being put on the sciatic nerve. Back pain, in general, is also very common, and something I experienced for most of my second pregnancy. Back pain can occur for any number of reasons, including increased hormones circulating your body, the increased weight from a growing bump, bad posture from your body changing, and even stress. I'm certain stress was a culprit for much of my back pain in my second pregnancy, as I was home taking care of another child and unable to rest when I really needed to.

Headaches are also very common in pregnancy. Like back pain, there are a lot of reasons why you might have these, including a rush of hormones and additional blood circulating your body. Be careful what you might use to alleviate pain from headaches because not all medications are safe during pregnancy! You will likely be able to get a list of approved medications from your doctor.

We've covered a lot of the seemingly normal and predictable aches and pains. Then there's a little thing my sister-in-law called 'lightning crotch' and it could not be more on point. I first experienced this lovely symptom when I was out on a walk after work one day. 'Lightning crotch' is exactly what it sounds like—your nerves lighting up like a lightning bolt straight through your lady parts. I imagine it is the pressure of your growing uterus hitting your nerves in just the right way, but it is some of the worst pain imaginable. I pray that you do not encounter this when you are a half-mile away from your couch because you will definitely want to walk as little as possible when the baby is in that particular position. The type of pain in your pelvic floor may not always be intense and sharp, but sometimes dull and aching, just due to all the pressure of your growing uterus and gravity.

Even things you think are supposed to be enjoyable during pregnancy can be painful. I'm willing to bet one of the best parts for most women is feeling their baby move. The first time you feel your baby is a little surreal. Like, you're not really sure whether you are getting ready to pass gas, or if you have popcorn popping in your stomach. It happens at different times for every woman, but the first time you feel it, it is surreal and elating at the same time. But fast forward to 7 months pregnant, and that once enjoyable baby movement might make you sick to your stomach. There is not a lot of room in the womb for a baby to grow, and they aren't just a little tadpole like your first sonogram. They grow limbs. And those limbs move. They move into your bladder, or your rib cage, and all your other organs. And sometimes they have really pointy elbows or sharp fists that drag all the way up and down your stomach like an alien waiting to break out of your skin. Those movements can be sharp and startling and painful. And then some women barely feel their babies move at all! Proving once again, that pregnancy is a very puzzling experience.

Whatever pains or strange symptoms you might be having during pregnancy, I will advise you of one thing. DO. NOT. GOOGLE IT. Google can certainly be a helpful tool if you're looking for nearby restaurants or someone to fix a broken pipe in your house, but just stay away from it when it comes to any kind of medical advice. I know you're going to do it anyway but also call a medical professional. Chances are, whatever you're experiencing is normal, and they can help put your mind at lease!

Other Weird Symptoms

There are likely some symptoms you already associate with pregnancy that you will not be surprised about. One of these is frequent urination. You have to pee ALL the time. It starts weirdly early in pregnancy, before you'd expect it to, because you aren't showing yet. Then as your uterus expands and your baby grows, there is less and less room for your bladder so the urge to pee might happen every 30 minutes. Maybe not that frequently, but it might feel like it, especially if you're pregnant during the summer and need to hydrate! Unfortunately, this need to pee doesn't stop when you sleep, either. You will be lucky to sleep uninterrupted at night because bathroom breaks are bound to happen. I'd usually get ready for bed, finally crawl in bed, then have to pee again, and then need to pee every three hours at night. I do drink a lot of water, but that bladder pressure is seriously no joke.

While we're talking about sleep, you might also experience

insomnia. We'll cover sleep as a separate chapter in the book, but pregnancy insomnia is a horrible, awful thing and there doesn't seem to be any good explanation for it. You might also experience vivid dreams. I have always been one to have strange dreams, but many women report very real dreams during their pregnancy. In-between insomnia pee breaks, I suppose.

Possibly the only benefit of being pregnant is that you don't get your period for about nine months. It seems awesome when you first think about it, right? Except, something almost worse happens instead. You will likely have a large amount of discharge during your pregnancy. It happens for various reasons, one of them is a hygiene mechanism your body uses to keep bacteria out of your vaginal canal as to not harm the growing fetus. I often had discharge so heavy it required wearing pads, which were more annoying than tampons during your period. That combined with sweat from your bump rubbing on your legs on a hot summer day will have you feeling like you always need to shower.

One of the most talked about, and possibly the weirdest, is food cravings. Pregnant women can crave some strange things. Before I got pregnant, I thought I might crave weird things, too, because it seems like you hear stories about food a lot. But it never really happened to me. I'd really crave burgers, citrusy food and salt—none of which are super out of the ordinary. There was no making my husband get out of bed at 11 pm to go to the store and buy Oreos and pickles type of cravings. Usually, you just crave what your body needs, and if you have a strong craving for sugar, maybe you just need carbs for energy!

Hot flashes and dizzy spells are other possible symptoms during pregnancy. I experienced these occasionally. If I had a dizzy spell, it was usually related to whether I'd eaten enough food or drank enough water. It's also much easier to get sick when you're pregnant, and there is a chance these symptoms could be related to a virus you've picked up. One night when I was pregnant with Charlotte, I spiked a 102-degree fever at midnight. I felt freezing, then had hot flashes and dizzy spells until the fever went away. For me personally, dizziness freaks me out. It's worth having a chat with your doctor about when you should give them a call if you're feeling sick or have a fever.

The Restrictions and Feelings

I'd title this chapter FOMO—fear of missing out—if it didn't make me sound like a complete alcoholic.

There are a lot of things you can't do while you're pregnant. Drinking and partying is obviously one of them. (I say obviously, but have you ever watched Mad Men? Oooh, the shit women did while pregnant in the 60s.) But there are many other things you just can't do. Restriction was one of the hardest things in pregnancy for me, mostly because I'm stubborn and I don't like outside circumstances dictating what I can and can't do. Even if it is my unborn baby holding me back from doing whatever it is that I think I want to be doing.

It starts with food. There are a lot of foods your doctor will advise you not to eat. Your immune system is compromised during pregnancy, and all the foods on the 'restricted' list are there because they could potentially make you sick. This was overall not too bad for me, because I didn't eat most of those foods anyway. But they tell you not to eat sandwich meat, and that one was tough! You'll find that there are workarounds for any of the foods you might be craving. Like sushi—you're not supposed to eat raw fish, but any of the cooked sushi is just fine. I'm a California roll girl myself, so this one was pretty easy. I will admit—I ate fresh deli turkey meat a couple of times and I was fine. That said, I think you should hear what your doctor has to say about it first, and then proceed at your own risk. All pregnancy circumstances are different!

Alright, so yes, drinking is something you can't do when you're pregnant. I complained about it a lot. I promise you that I am not an alcoholic, and I gave up drinking with ease during pregnancy. I could give up drinking under other normal circumstances in my life, too. But I am constantly invited to be a part of activities that typically involve people drinking. Depending on what stage you are in life, partying or going to bars may or may not be something you will actually miss. I'd say that for the first half of my pregnancies, drinking sounded awful and not something I even wanted to do because I either didn't feel well, or I was so damn tired. But in that last trimester, when your belly is big, and you're overheated and cranky, a glass of wine might sound better than ever in that moment.

It's not always the actual drinking of alcohol that gives me a bit of FOMO. It's more feeling like I belong. I love to be social, and a lot of the time that involves drinking socially. For some reason, for me, being pregnant made me feel really out of place, like an outsider, in a lot of situations. I was in one of my best friend's weddings during my first pregnancy. We rode on a party bus between the ceremony and reception. The wedding party had a blast, while I dodged champagne corks and people falling on top of me. Definitely felt like an outsider and missed the vodka during that one. Oh, and the time I went to Colorado on St. Patrick's Day weekend for a bachelorette party and went with all the girls to a dispensary. Actually, I just sat outside on the curb for that one because a pregnant woman in a weed store is just too weird. Also, the smell made me want to vom. The drunk girl sitting next to me must have thought the same thing as she stumbled over to the trash can on the street corner to let it out.

It was hard for me to go anywhere trying to look decent without feeling frumpy and uncomfortable. This was all in my head and not a result of anyone's actions toward me, but it was how I felt and sometimes you can't help how you feel.

The number of physical things you shouldn't do during pregnancy can sometimes outnumber the 'restricted' list you'll receive from your doctor. While skiing during a winter trip to Colorado in my first pregnancy was on my doctor's 'no' list, taking a boat ride in the summer wasn't, but I couldn't do that either because hitting any waves was very uncomfortable. Sitting outside in the summer for an extended period of time was impossible because I'd quickly overheat and get sunburnt. I was never told I shouldn't work out but working out was tough and sometimes painful.

Missing out on superficial things during pregnancy is going to happen. We know this. But you might also miss out on really important things. Towards the end of your pregnancy, one of the 'restricted' activities is traveling. When I was 35 weeks pregnant with Brooklyn, my grandpa passed away. I had missed my grandma's funeral, and I really wanted to go. I had connected with family to construct plans. I was overwhelmed with old pictures and stories about my grandparents shared online. One of those pictures was a family photo from the previous Christmas, and in it was my dad. My dad and I had an estranged relationship at the time, which is another topic in another book, but he was an addict and he had cancer; he never took care of himself and it was a very toxic situation. So, I removed myself from it. But my heart wrenched when I saw that photo of him because he looked so old. He looked older than my grandpa. I couldn't believe it and I was dead set on going to that funeral so I could grieve with my family, but also see my dad.

I am from Wisconsin, and most of my family lives there. We live in Texas. At 35 weeks pregnant, it was too late in pregnancy to fly. So, I started planning a road trip with my husband and my sister. It sounds batshit crazy, right? A woman who is 5 weeks from giving birth, sitting in a car for 18 hours, one way? It never occurred to me that I shouldn't go, until Kyle asked me to clear it with my doctor. You won't be surprised to find out that my doctor, although he couldn't explicitly tell me no, strongly advised against it.

So, there I was, super pregnant and hormonal, crying about pretty much everything in my life that lead me to that moment. Pregnancy is not just restriction from superficial things, although I pray you don't miss some of your important moments. Since I couldn't go, I paid tribute to my grandpa, who was an artist, by making artwork for Brooklyn's room. And I called my dad and I ended our estrangement because I couldn't imagine having a grandchild that he wouldn't meet.

Going to that funeral seemed like the most important thing at the time. But ultimately, what truly is most important is keeping your baby safe. Once you have that baby, all the pain and sickness and sacrifice from pregnancy are forgotten, but it can be hard to live with when you're in it.

And the FOMO. The FOMO will be worth it, too.

Most of the contents of this chapter are things I didn't know about before I got pregnant. It's hard to pin down just one thing I wish I had known because ultimately it wouldn't have made a difference. I'd have still gotten pregnant. And I'd probably would have still hated it. In conversation with other women, here are some things they wish they had known.

- How quickly it goes by, even if each day passes slowly.
- I wish I knew how much being pregnant sucks! It was like a 40-week hangover.
- That I'd experience pain in the most random places throughout my body—and early on in my pregnancy. As soon as one area started to feel better, something else would start hurting.
- The pelvic floor pain was unbearable.
- Morning sickness is actually all-day sickness.
- That stretching and pre-natal yoga can help with pain—I didn't know this until my second pregnancy.
- Not only how bad I felt in the first trimester, but the hunger swings and aversions to food. I was plant-based for over three years, and the only thing I could eat was chicken breast.

4 PREPARING FOR BABY

Believe it or not, there are some tactical things you'll read in an ordinary parenting book that can help prepare you for living with a baby. But don't read about them there, read about them here instead. Because this is tactical, but it is also practical. There are things you really 'need' to do or purchase to raise a baby, and there are things that you really don't. But damn if they don't make your life more convenient.

<u>The Registry</u>

To prepare for a baby, you're going to need to buy stuff. And there can be a lot of stuff. It's actually amazing that our parents were ever able to raise us without all this stuff. If the zombie apocalypse ever happens, I am certain the human race would die out. Not because we can't kill zombies, but because there is no way we could raise a baby without our precious mechanical bassinets and formula machines and cuddly, glowing nightlights.

Most of the time, there is someone in your life who will offer to throw you a baby shower. And to do that, you'll probably create a baby registry. Completing a baby registry is utterly overwhelming. Have you ever walked into a Buy Buy Baby before? You don't have kids yet, so probably not. It's an entire department store JUST for babies. How is it possible that such tiny little humans can demand SO much stuff?

My ultimate tip for you when completing your registry is NOT to bring your husband when you do this. Instead, bring a friend who has already had a baby. Trust me, you and your husband will both thank me for this piece of advice. Your husband would probably rather do anything else besides walk through a baby store with a handheld scanner listening to you say, 'Do you think we need this?' 500 times, only to result in him shrugging his shoulders saying 'Sure?' He will be so appreciative that he might even give you a foot massage because you spent two hours walking around a store while he watched Netflix.

When I say there is a lot of stuff you can buy for a baby, I am not exaggerating. The number of gadgets and brands that are almost exactly the same, but in different colored boxes is maddening. But it is a market that is never going away (ya know, until we hit the zombie apocalypse) and people are willing to buy whatever it takes to make their lives more convenient.

I can't say I haven't done it. It's inevitable you're going to buy more than you need because you want to buy cute stuff for your baby. You're excited for your baby and want your baby to look adorable at all times (not like they need extra things for that!). There's nothing wrong with making your baby fashionable with headbands or bowties and you push them around in a stroller that costs more than what my 2010 Ford Fusion is worth. I'm not saying you shouldn't do those things if you don't want to. Just know you don't HAVE to. I don't believe you need all those things. You just need the right things, so you don't waste a lot of money. You should start with the basics, and then figure out if any of the fancy contraptions on the market are something you'll want before you buy them, and your baby doesn't like them anyway. Because that happens, too.

The Essentials

This list will be too minimalistic for some of you, but I think these are the absolute essentials you'd need for a baby. If you're on a tight budget, forget the matching crib sets and the cute animal print artwork. Register for this stuff first.

Diapers You'll go through a lot of newborn diapers. Yes, newborn specific diapers exist. They are teeny tiny. And guess what? Not a lot of brands make them, and they're the most expensive kind you can buy. Diapers come in many other different sizes, and all brands have sizes ranging from 1 through 6. I remember registering for diapers and my friend was all like, add a bunch of all these sizes. And I felt like an idiot because I wondered, "How do I know when a baby needs a new size? All the clothes tell me what size based on the month, and I can look at a calendar to figure that out." The size of diaper your baby will wear is based on your baby's weight. Underneath the size number on the box will be a weight range that you can use as a gauge. Although if your baby has poop that leaks out of the diaper multiple times in one day, that's also a good sign you need to go up a size.

Wipes No real explanation necessary. Although I am a big proponent of generating minimal waste, diapers and wipes are just not an area of my life I'm willing to sacrifice in the disposable waste department. Register for a big box of refillable packs, not a bunch of small packs. And if you have a membership to a store like Costco or Sam's Club, buy them there. You'll save a ton of money.

Diaper cream There's a ridiculous number of diaper creams on the market, and most of them are the exact same. Take a look at the 'active ingredient' on a few of them to understand how they differ. I have found that knockoffs do just as good a job as the name brand. You'll find some cream-based kinds with Zinc Oxide (brands like Desitin), or some petroleum-based kinds (brands like Aquaphor). The petroleum kinds are the same thing as Vaseline—no other active ingredients that do anything different than lube up your baby's bottom. Literally, Aquaphor can charge 8 times the price because it's in a tube instead of a jar, and it says 'for baby' on the packaging. You might want to get a few different kinds of creams. Different creams work better or worse for different babies. Zinc Oxide worked for one of my babies and Vaseline worked for the other.

Sleepers with zippers My husband would 100% vouch for this one. My babies basically lived in their pajamas until they were two months old. I don't know if you've ever tried to dress a baby in pants and a shirt before, but it's a pain in the ass. They're super floppy, their arms are rubbery and usually, clothing is either way too big or way too small.

The key to this recommendation, though, is the zipper. Zippers on sleepers are critical. When you're tired, trying to connect 20+ snaps on the clothing of a newborn who is wailing and flailing is what nightmares are made of. Don't do that to yourself.

Velcro or zippered swaddle I applaud the parents who have mastered the swaddle blanket, but I don't have time for that. Velcro swaddles are foolproof to use, and ninja-babies have a harder time breaking out of them. Sometimes an arm busting out can ruin your entire night. Baby straight-jacket for the win!

Crib While you probably will want to get some kind of bouncing or rocking seat to put your baby in so you're not holding them all day (nothing against moms who want to hold their babies all day, but I am not that mom), a crib is obviously for sleeping. We never bought a bassinet or any of the fancy in-room sleeping machines (something called the Snoo just came out, it looks fancy). Our babies slept in the crib from day one. There are multiple benefits to this that we can discuss in a later chapter.

Mattress cover and sheets It might not seem like babies will need their bedding changed very often, but you might be surprised. Spit up is most common, but occasionally you'll get a leaky poop that gives you a nice surprise in the middle of the night. Most crib mattresses have plastic coatings, so mattress covers aren't always necessary, but they do help to absorb any spit up and prevent a bigger mess. Keep two mattress covers in rotation and a few crib sheets handy. There might be nights when you go through them all!

Rocking Chair Chairs can come in a drastic range of prices. We decided to splurge in the chair department. But you're going to have to make a serious decision and choose between aesthetics and comfort. You can probably guess what I decided to go with… I refused to get a chair that in any way resembled a La-Z-Boy. So, we searched for months to find a chair that was suitable for my taste and found an over-stuffed swivel and rocking chair. We paid $700 for it. I loved the pattern and the style. Having a chair that swiveled AND rocked was pretty clutch. (Do people still say this?) But it didn't recline, which in hindsight probably would have been nice (according to my husband), although you can't recline and rock at the same time. Also, the cushion was really annoying and would slide out all the time. Almost every time I sat on it, I thought about adding Velcro underneath the seat. Which, I never did before we sold it over three years later. My advice? Determine your budget and then go sit in a bunch of chairs and see if any of them annoy you more or less than others. Try not to get too hung up on what it looks like, unless you want to open up your budget.

Low-light source Whether it is a lamp or a dimmable overhead light, having a low-light source will help with nighttime feedings. Blasting a bright light may wake and startle your little one in the middle of the night. Ideally, you can keep them sleepy so that after their feed, you'll be able to get some more sleep, too!

Car seat Oof. Choosing a car seat can be mind-boggling because there are so many on the market. I can see how this would easily be a stressful decision because it is the ultimate baby-safety purchase. I have never been someone who wants to research products before I buy them and reading reviews on car seats sounded miserable. Wanna know what I did? I bought the same one my best friend had. They did lots of research. She liked it, so I figured I'd like it, too. And I did! What you'll find is that so many car seats are very similar, but they have different ways of attaching to strollers, pulling straps, adjusting headrests, etc. My only advice would be to find a car seat with a strap adjustment in the front and not the back. Much more convenient that way!

Stroller I did not know this when I looked for a stroller, but for newborns, the easiest thing to do is find a stroller that has some kind of frame that will fit your car seat. All car seat brands come with their own types of frames that are compatible, and you just clip the car seat into the frame. It's quite easy. The basic frames themselves are usually not too expensive. You start getting into pricy territory when you're looking at jogging strollers. (Side note: there is a specific age when you are able to run with your baby. Their neck has to be strong enough to support all the bouncing. Check with your pediatrician on the recommended age!) You can get into even pricier territory looking at high-end stroller brands. Yes, they exist. They look sleek, and I have heard they can be easier to use and have lots of convertible parts you can buy for different seating options. I think they are supposed to have good safety standards. I don't really know any of these things for sure because there was no way I was paying $1,000 for a stroller. Especially not when a car seat fits pretty perfectly inside the shopping carts at Target. Just sayin'.

Sound machine The magic of white noise is straight out of Hogwarts. Sound machines can also be really expensive. Some double as projectors or nightlights, but ultimately the sound is what you really need. If you have an iPad or an old iPhone/iPod laying around (I don't know if anyone has iPods anymore, they're basically prehistoric), you can use that with a white noise app if you want to save some money.

Bottles Some people will tell you to register for multiple types of bottles. I'm not one of those people. We found that our babies took to the first type of bottle we gave them without issue. We even switched bottles a couple of times with Charlotte to try and manage her colic but ended up using the ones we started with. The difference for us may have been that they were on bottles very early, and not solely breastfed for months before. If you do register for multiple bottles, do not open them and make sure to save the receipts. There is a good chance you'll be able to stick with the first kind you try.

Whichever bottles you do try, though, look for bottle nipples that are very slow flow. Do some research to find the slowest flow nipple possible for your baby. We used Tommee Tippee zero-flow nipples that worked well for our girls. Babies spill a lot when they drink from a bottle (see 'Bibs' below). Like diapers, there are sure signs when you need to up the nipple flow. If your baby looks red in the face or appears to be sucking super hard, up that flow.

Bottle brush and foaming soap Cleaning bottles and all the parts that come along with them can be tricky. Having a bottle cleaning brush will help that. There are some baby-specific foaming soaps you can buy which are fragrance-free, but you can probably find cheaper alternative foaming soaps you are comfortable with using. The foaming soap is easier to use than regular dish soap since you don't have the lathering ability when using a brush. Even though hand-washing bottles is more work, you might be better off doing it that way as opposed to using a dishwasher. We bought one of those traps that hold bottle parts to run in the top rack of the dishwasher. The bottles and nipples got a weird film on them after running them in the dishwasher a few times, so we stopped using it. A friend once told me that she and her husband alternate everything they do with their kids, down to taking turns washing the bottles every other day. I think it's a great idea. Even the simplest chores can add up with your kiddos!

Formula Even if you are absolutely determined to breastfeed your baby from the start, it's never a bad idea to have formula on hand. There are times when you might unexpectedly need it. I have a friend who got really sick a couple months after giving birth, and she was placed on antibiotics so she couldn't breastfeed. They were forced to start formula before they were ready. Making a decision about a newborn or infant formula you want to have on hand could help reduce a little anxiety if you encounter a similar stressful situation.

Pacifiers Pacifiers are weird, and babies don't always like whatever ones you buy. There's also a lot of weird names for these, and I honestly didn't realize they could be called a 'pacifier' until I had a baby. We called them a 'nuk,' which is actually a brand name. Kyle and his family all called them a 'bink,' which makes no real sense to me. Lots of people call them 'pacis.' Again, on-trend for us, Charlotte was much pickier with basically everything than Brooklyn decided to be. I originally bought the same kind of pacifiers that Brooklyn had, and she rejected them. Luckily, they're cheap and people will probably randomly buy these for you anyway, so you'll have a few different kinds laying around.

Blankets Don't buy them—at least not until after your baby is born. There is a weird unwritten rule that you will receive a lot of baby blankets as gifts. The only thing you might consider is some lightweight swaddle blankets. We bought these and never really used them for Brooklyn, but we use them all the time with Charlotte. Difference between a spring and fall baby perhaps.

Bibs If you're going to bottle feed, you'll definitely need some bibs. Newborn babies are not efficient when they drink from a bottle. It can be particularly painful if you're losing a lot of hard-earned breastmilk or formula that costs $1.50 per scoop. You can alleviate spillage with slow flow nipples, but even the slowest flow might not be slow enough for a newborn. They will eventually get the hang of it. Until they do, you'll go through a lot of bibs in one day, because they can get soaked. And after using them twice, they start to smell really bad. Formula does not smell good when it's mixed up and heated (babies must not have taste buds), and it smells even worse after it's seeped into a bib and sat around on a couch for a few hours. Bibs were the main reason I did so much laundry during the newborn days. At least one load of laundry every single day! And if you run out of bibs, don't worry, you can get resourceful. I once used an extra pair of pajamas as a bib on a flight to Indiana because all the bibs I did pack were checked in our luggage.

Changing pad Getting a changing pad is definitely helpful, but I am not necessarily saying you need to buy an entire changing table. We got a free changing table, so we had one, but I am not sure we'd have bought one otherwise. In hindsight, you only use it for about 8-9 months before you give up and start changing diapers on the floor. Babies quickly outgrow a standard changing pad. The length of your baby isn't necessarily the issue, either. It's the kicking and flailing that makes changing on the table a bit of a challenge. The floor serves as a much more convenient and less dangerous table. If you want a changing table, then, by all means, buy one! But if you have the ability to set up some kind of convertible station, like a changing pad on top of a dresser, I would recommend going that route. So long as you feel it's safe enough to use!

And remember don't ever leave your baby unattended on their changing table. Not leaving them alone, or never removing a hand from them, makes it easier to change then on something not meant to be a changing table. I have a friend whose baby chose an unattended moment at the changing table to learn to roll. That would be a scary moment.

Changing pad covers and liners You'll be shocked the first time you see a projectile poop. It is amazing how much force can erupt from the bottom of such a tiny human. These are necessary sanitary purchases. Make sure to have at least 1-2 back-ups.

Diaper pail I definitely considered adding this as a 'convenience' item and not an essential one. Technically you could just throw your baby's diapers in the trash or keep them in a pail in the garage. But after thinking about it, baby poop can smell really bad, especially once you switch to formula. And even worse when you switch to pureed food. Again, there are several types on the market, some that use bag refills and some that don't, so take a look at what is best for you.

Soft teething toy I hesitate to add this as an 'essential' item because babies will chew on just about anything you give them. But this isn't something you'll want to buy used, so let's go ahead and throw it on here. Babies teethe at a very wide range of ages, so these could be of benefit for you earlier than expected.

Diaper bag You are going to want some kind of diaper bag, but I don't think you need to buy something that is sold as a diaper bag. Diaper bags are glorified tote purses that aren't always designed the best. An oversized tote bag works great to cart around your baby's essentials. You can also find backpacks, too. Either a backpack sold as a diaper bag, or a new stylish one you find at Target (maybe I shop there a lot, can you tell yet?). Or even a sports backpack because they have lots of pockets and places to stash things. Anything hands-off is always helpful.

Nail clipper Clipping your child's nails is one of the hardest jobs on the planet, but unless you want your baby to turn into a velociraptor, you need to do it. They make nail clippers that are small for their tiny fingers. Some of them have a little hole so you can see if you're just getting a nail or also about to clip their skin off. Not sure how you'd ever be able to use that though, because it wasn't until my daughter turned 2 that she wasn't flailing like a maniac any time I pulled out a nail clipper. Just had to clip and hope for the best!

Thermometers I hope that you don't need to use one of these early on in your baby's life, but they are good to have at home. There are two types of thermometers you can buy: a rectal thermometer and a contact thermometer. You have to use a rectal thermometer to take a newborn's temperature because it is the most accurate place. The other thermometers are contact, so you can take the temperature on their forehead. Check with your doctor on when it is appropriate to switch from the rectal to a contact thermometer.

Safety swabs The most random thing on the list, but it is a recommended and overlooked item. I actually didn't register for this the first time, but they were gifted to me anyway. They are cotton swabs to clean your baby's ears, but they have a large end do you can't stick them too far in and damage their eardrums.

Something to suck snot out of your kids nose You'll use this more than you prefer. Typically, the hospital will send you home with a small ball sucker intended for newborn spit up. You can buy these at the store if you need an extra. There are also straws on the market now used to literally suck the snot out of your kid's nose. With your mouth. It sounds disgusting, but it works so well, you'll never go back. You won't get sick either, I promise. Google it!

Gift cards Because you'll always be buying more stuff, and you won't really know what other stuff you need until you actually need it.

Other Items to Consider

Some of these I think are more 'nice to have' items on your registry because you won't actually need them immediately. There may also be alternatives to each item and a lot of these you can seek out second hand to save yourself a lot of money.

Yes, adding them to a registry means that someone might buy them for you brand new. But remember—you can have people buying you diapers, wipes, and other absolute essentials that are more expensive than finding gently-used baby seats and toys! To put all these items in perspective, I am going to provide a duration of time that we actually used these them. It may help you decide what you want to source second hand. Or perhaps you'll have friends who had these for their first child, aren't currently using, and are holding for their second child. You could ask to borrow it and give it back when you're done! My friends and I did this, and it was incredibly helpful.

Baby Monitor (duration: from birth to toddler) Remember that many of our parents raised us without baby monitors at all. This is not something you must have, at least not right away, and especially if baby is sleeping in the room with you. A newborn baby's cry is piercing. Unless you have a massive house, chances are you will hear your baby cry wherever you are at. Our newborns slept straight in the crib. In our first house, we didn't even really need a monitor because with our bedroom door open, we were able to hear her cry from her room and it would wake us up. For our second baby, we were in a new house, and we had to close our door so our dog wouldn't come in and wake us up. (His nails on the floors sounded like a horse.) We used a monitor for baby two right away but kept the sound up only enough so we could hear her real cry and not hear all the grunting that sleeping babies usually make!

I have mixed feelings about using the cameras on baby monitors. They don't really become necessary until your baby is really mobile. In today's world, though, healthcare professionals put a large emphasis on preventing SIDS (sudden infant death syndrome). I think this creates a lot more paranoia than there needs to be. Some days, I am care-free about the camera, and some days I stare at it for five minutes to just 'make sure' my baby is breathing. It's silly, but I do it anyway. If all we had was an audio monitor, we would be just fine!

Traditional baby monitors are more expensive than other app-based camera systems that you can find. There are some on the market that are very affordable, and you can download the corresponding app to your phone instead of carrying around a second monitor. We went the app-based route and it was a great decision.

Activity mat (duration: newborn to 6 months) We used the activity mat a lot. Although it is not 'essential' it is something I would recommend buying. It gives you a place to lay your baby and gives them something to look at. They begin to interact and play with the overhead toys. We would lay our babies on this as soon as 2 weeks, and we used it until they could properly sit on their own.

Lounger (duration: birth to 7 months) There are so many different types of loungers or chairs you can get for baby. Types that rock or bounce. If you do buy one, do just that—buy only one. Chances are you'd use one way more than the rest, and the result will be a clutter of baby seats you stub your toes on every day.

Jumper (duration: 4-7 months) Baby jumpers are expensive, and babies aren't really that hard on them so you should be able to find a decent second-hand option. You also aren't going to set this up until your baby is 4-5 months old at the earliest, so it's one less thing crowding a closet until you need it.

Swing (duration: newborn to 8 months) Some babies love the swing, and some babies do not. This could be an unfortunate thing to learn if you dropped a lot of money on one.

Baby Countertop Seat (duration: 4-6 months) Although you don't use this one for very long, it is incredibly helpful. Most babies don't sit very well on their own for a while, and these seats give them support to help them do that. Some doctors recommend starting small amounts of baby foods before they're able to sit up on their own, so these types of seats make that possible. You can find seats that sit on top of the counter or seats that can strap on to a countertop. The seats that strap on to a counter are better for travel. We were lucky to receive both kinds from a friend after their kids were done with them!

High Chair (duration: 6-18 months) There are some high chairs that look really nice and cost a lot more. But the fact is, they are going to get incredibly disgusting after a short time. Yes, you can wash them, but it's nearly impossible not to get baby food purees smeared in the crevices of the joints and screws. We have a $25 high chair from Walmart that works just fine! Unless it is very gently used, this is not an item I'd recommend buying second-hand.

Booster Seat (duration: 18-24 months) A booster seat will strap onto the chair at your kitchen table to be used in place of the high chair. I've found this is an item some kids don't want to use. They'd rather use the high chair, or just sit in the 'big kid' chair! We bought this but didn't end up using it for very long at all, only until 20 months.

Solid food feeding supplies (duration: 4 months +) Spoons, plates, bowls and cups. You won't use these for a while, so you may hold off on purchasing any of these until you're ready.

Toys (3 months +) Registering for some basic rattles and young toys is something you might do. Babies don't have the skills to play with anything until 3-4 months old at the earliest. Before then, an activity mat will suffice as playtime! I would not register for much else or buy anything else until you feel your child is ready for it. That gives you time to decide how many additional toys/things you want to add to your life. You're also bound to receive toys as gifts, whether it be at birth or a birthday.

A baby wrap (duration: newborn–1 year) Baby wearing is all the rage. It can be a lifesaver if you have a fussy newborn. Or if you just want to get shit done. But I would not recommend buying a baby wrap until you've actually tried one on. There is a variety of brands and styles. Some that have clips and some that involve ninja-skills to put on your body. Truth is though, you might not like wearing it, or your baby might not like being in it. I would seek out moms who own them and source as many opinions about baby wraps as you can. Then, see if you'd be able to borrow one for a day, or even stop over for an afternoon to try it on. I've also seen them hanging out for try-on at some stores (like Target). I tried twice to wear one of those super-long wraps that I literally had to find a YouTube tutorial for each time. It was awful and I found a new one that was a good blend between wrap and clip-on, super comfortable, and worked well for my baby. But I wouldn't have known that when I was pregnant because you can't wear them with a big old bump of a belly!

Portable playard (duration: newborn–2 years) There are several brands of portable playards, but Pack 'n Play is the most common brand and is often used as a noun just like Crock-pot is used in place of slow cooker. I say that because without calling it a Pack 'n Play, you probably wouldn't know what it was called. I have lovingly referred to it as the 'baby cage,' which is not really politically correct. Does the same thing though? The playard is great if you know you will be traveling a lot to places that don't have cribs. I can probably count on both hands the number of times we've actually used it in the first two years of Brooklyn's life. We'd take it over to friends' houses for social gatherings, and it was available for use for our friends' and families' children when they visit. Although you could check it on a flight if you're traveling, it is just an extra thing to haul around. If you are traveling and staying in a hotel somewhere, call ahead to see if they have any cribs available. Several hotels do! These playards cost anywhere from $50 to $200, so purchase at your own discretion.

Boppy or other breastfeeding pillow (duration: newborn–5 months) Boppy is the most common brand for breastfeeding pillows, though breastfeeding is not their only function. They can also be used as support for your baby practicing tummy time or sitting up. We sometimes propped our babies in it for bottle feeding so we didn't need to hold them, which helped us free one hand until they could hold the bottle on their own. I found it uncomfortable for breastfeeding. We used it for bottle feeding more often with Brooklyn than Charlotte. I think this is a completely optional purchase.

Bassinet (duration: newborn–3 months) You do not need a bassinet. You do not need to have your baby sleeping in your room with you. We never did. Our babies slept straight in the crib from the first day they were home! That said, I understand not all mothers are comfortable with this arrangement. And depending on whether you are breastfeeding or bottle feeding, one sleeping arrangement might be more convenient than another. Brooklyn slept through the night early, and I attribute that in part to her being in her crib. Charlotte had long stretches early as well, but we battled lots of colic and teething with her, so she was consistently sleeping all night around six to seven months. Moving a baby to a crib may be an abrupt change in routine for them if they are used to getting snug in a bassinet, Rock 'n Play, or another type of lounger. As always, do what is best for you, and know that there is not one single way you need to put your baby to sleep.

Clothing While you obviously need to clothe your baby, do not overdo it with clothing early on in their life. Clothing sizes are not consistent between brands, and at times even among brands. Some items will last much longer than you expect based on the intended month size. Also, babies all grow at different paces, so your three-month-old baby could very well be wearing six-months clothing, and vice versa. Because of these reasons, you could end up with a wardrobe of unseasonal clothing if you buy too much in advance. I highly recommend seeking out second-hand clothing. Oftentimes, especially for babies, it is gently used. Just like blankets, you're also likely to be gifted clothing. Keep the cute outfits, and then donate the stuff you don't like. Just kidding! Keep the stuff you don't like for extra outfits at daycare when they poop or spit up all over their clothes. Still functional, but they aren't often seen or photographed in it. Win, win!

Baby bath or seat (duration: newborn–7 months) Depending on your bathroom situation, you may or may not need one of these. If all you have is a stand-up shower, then you'll want to seek out an easy option for bathing your child. There are many different types of baths on the market. I have seen baby shower seats be very successful until they can sit in the bath on their own! A laundry basket is also appropriate. There are special baths for newborns, but not all newborn babies like the bath, so spending money on something you don't use much might not be your thing. Alternatives to a newborn bath are easy—roll up a towel to prop them on in the kitchen sink.

I also follow a blogger who lives in a small townhome in Boston, and she uses an Ikea trash can (don't worry, I don't think it's ever been used for trash) for her son and he loves the crap out of it. Also seems pretty convenient. So, there are lots of options in this category.

Washcloths These are also probably unnecessary but having small washcloths for baby is easier than using a regular one. You don't need many and they're fairly cheap. I don't see much use in bath towels made for baby, because a towel you'd use works exactly the same. We would not have bought one if we weren't given one off-registry.

Things You Probably Don't Need

Now that we've covered the things I recommend getting, let's cover the things I think you can skip.

Matching crib sets In all reality, matching crib sets are not practical. Doctors will tell you that your babies can't sleep with a blanket until they're about one. Really, you'll be able to tell when they can or can't sleep with a blanket, because you're the ones watching them sleep. They just need to be strong enough so they can't get tangled in it and suffocate. Brooklyn started sleeping with cuddly things and light blankets at naptime at 10 months old. But matching crib sets are really expensive, and as mentioned, you'll likely get gifted a few blankets anyways. Instead of the crib sets, get a bunch of sets of sheets. Those you will probably go through quickly. You can also find lots of cute patterns for sheets, so your nursey doesn't need to look drab without the matching blanket.

Crib liner This item is more irritating than it is helpful, at least in the early months of your baby's life. Crib mattresses are designed to fit very snuggly inside a crib so that babies can't get their hands or feet stuck. When you have a crib liner installed, it makes it really difficult to change sheets on the crib mattress. We put this liner on the crib for both babies and took it off within a couple of months. The only reason you might need this is if your baby rolls around a lot in their sleep, causing them to bump their head on the crib and wake up. You might want to hold off on purchasing this to see if your child even needs one.

Bottle warmer I am a little hypocritical putting this on the 'don't buy' list because with Charlotte we bought a Baby Brezza, which is an expensive formula machine that measures and makes bottles at perfect drinking temperature. But the Baby Brezza was completely worth the money in how much time it saved. A regular bottle warmer is not. They take a lot of time to heat up a bottle, and five minutes can feel like an eternity with a screaming baby. I will not lie to you. Before that, we used a microwave. To either heat water before mixing formula or *gasp* even to reheat formula bottles. Yes, we reheated some formula! Yes, it is faux pas but my kids are alive and healthy and sometimes recommendations don't make any sense. (We didn't reuse any formula that sat out longer than recommended.)

Bottle drying rack These are pricy, and they don't hold a lot of items. I'd recommend finding a cheaper drying mat to sit all your bottles and bottle parts on. It works just as well, and it is easy to throw in the wash once a week!

Multiple bottle types We used only one bottle in an entire year. Register for one bottle. Let people spend their money on other more necessary things.

Multiple baby wash types You will more than likely get some kind of care package that has baby wash in it. We were gifted three bottles of baby wash, and four years later, we still have not had to purchase more!

A mobile We never used it. It got in the way when Brooklyn could pull up and she'd just hang on it. We had one that played music and the battery died within 6 months, and we couldn't change it out. Pretty much a waste of money.

Anything for making baby food You ain't got time for that. Or may you do, or you'll make time for it, but you'll be a long way off from even needing ot make the decision when your baby is born. It sounds like a grand idea when you're completing a registry or dreaming of the all-natural supermom you're going to be. I would call myself pretty 'natural,' and I don't have time to make baby food. I tried once and I laugh at myself for how much effort it took! If you are waste-conscious like me, purchase baby food in glass bottles with metal lids that can be recycled instead of the plastic containers with film lids.

A baby care kit We registered for one of these and we only used the nail clipper, thermometer and the comb from it. They usually come with lots of other little things you'll have anyway. They also come with a squeeze ball to suck boogers out of your kid's nose, but the hospital will usually send you home with one of those.

Things That Other Mothers Swear You Need

I polled other women about one thing they'd recommend new parents add to their registry. This is what they came up with.

- A handheld vacuum
- The swaddles that zip up
- Gerber Soothe probiotics
- Ubbi Diaper Pail—doesn't require special bags, and prevents smelling from dirty diapers
- Baby swing
- Gas drops

- A tiered cart on wheels to store all necessities that can be wheeled around from room to room

The Nursery

Decorating the nursery was my favorite part of pregnancy.

I had dreams of a perfect nursery. I've always preferred that the space I live in be as aesthetically pleasing as possible. My hidden 'baby girl' Pinterest board was filled with nursery ideas, color schemes and fun artwork I could buy.

It ended up being adorable. Kyle spent time installing a board and batten look. I did some of my own painting for artwork in her room. I found a tufted toy chest on sale at Marshall's, and we found a nice second-hand crib and dresser. The paint color ended up not being what I wanted (was going for mint, and it ended up way too bright). Lesson learned on not testing out an actual paint sample before you hire people to paint.

The nursery was wonderful, but I ended up spending a lot more time and energy and money on it than we originally anticipated. And the kicker is, we hardly spent any time in that room outside of nighttime feedings. Even as Brooklyn grew up, she played more in the family room than her own room.

Most of our time was, and still is, spent in the common areas of our home. Who wants to go into a secluded room to play with baby? We did not. We ended up moving the toy chest out to the living room, where it didn't really fit, but we had invested in this thing and it was functional, so we weren't spending money on something else.

Like organizing during nesting, the nursery is a space that you wouldn't know how you want to use it until you're actually using it. If you're like me and you MUST have the nursery completely decorated and 'done' before baby, then have at it. But know that it's totally okay to be up in the air about plans for baby's room. I bet many of you will end up having baby sleep in your room for 1-3 months anyway. That's a lot of time for a nursery to be perfectly laid out and unused!

The most important thing about your nursery is that it should be a calming space. If you have boxes of clothes or diapers you need to unpack, stash them in a closet somewhere. Get rid of the clutter. Have a lamp, a sound machine, and some soft blankets for you and for baby. Get cozy in a chair. If you're trying to feed your baby in the nursery, or wanting them to sleep there, having a calm space will help you feel calm. And if you feel calm, your baby has a better chance at it, too!

Don't get caught up on whether your nursery is Pinterest-perfect. It's a stress you don't need. And it will end up being a space you'll invest in that you won't really use much anyway!

If we want to be practical, here is a list of things that you should have in your nursery when baby is born:

- Crib
- Lamp
- Chair of choice (see The Registry)
- Sound machine
- Nightlight
- Place to stash baby's sleepers and clothes

<u>Nesting</u>

You will hear about this thing called nesting. People would ask me in my first pregnancy whether I was nesting yet. I took offense to it sometimes because I took offense to a lot of dumb things when I was pregnant, mostly because I was so stubborn about hating pregnancy that I didn't want to admit I was enjoying anything that came along with it.

Nesting is this weird urge to get shit done. And I loooooove getting shit done. Just ask my husband about my to-do lists. Nesting was kind of awesome for me, because it was an excuse to check things off my list, and officially claim we were ready for baby.

Getting your house in perfect working order before baby is quite comical in an ironic sort of way because your house and sometimes your life are literal disasters not long after you bring home your bundle of joy. And if you organize things before you are actually using them, you're bound to realize your systems don't work the way you hope and that you need to have diapers on the left side of the changing table instead of the right side. But having some kind of system in place can be much more calming than walking into chaos for your first night home with baby.

While you're running about your house organizing the dishwasher tabs under the sink, I encourage you to do a thorough purge of stuff you no longer use. I am recently becoming a fan of 'minimalism,' which isn't just living a life in a white room with one couch and one set of silverware. It's about keeping only the things that provide function and value to you. Many people can live 'out of sight, out of mind,' but if I know my closets and cabinets are busting at the seams every time that I open them, I might go a little berserk. Remember that you're about to bring new things into your home for baby. My advice is to get rid of things you don't use or forgot you even had, so your home doesn't explode with the addition of all things baby.

Choosing a Pediatrician

This is something you'll need to check off your list before your baby is born. When you fill out your hospital paperwork, you'll need to provide them with your selected pediatrician. Once baby exits the womb, the hospital will notify your pediatrician and they will send the on-call doctor to examine your little one. If for whatever reason you don't list a pediatrician, the hospital will still have your newborn cared for after birth.

It is not usually required that you meet a pediatrician before you select one. You will, however, need to make sure that their office is accepting new patients. There is no paperwork to fill out ahead of time, so the process is fairly simple.

Going to a new doctor yourself for the first time can be uneasy, so choosing one for your baby can feel very important. If you feel lost in selecting one, talk to people in your area who have children. If you don't have any friends with kids, find a coworker or neighbor and see where they go. We selected our pediatrician off a friend's recommendation.

<u>Childcare</u>

Childcare is another important decision you need to nail down. How long will you stay home with your baby? Will you enroll them in daycare or get a nanny? If you choose daycare, will you look for an in-home or a franchise option? I am certainly not going to judge anyone for what they think is right for their family. There are benefits and disadvantages to anything you do. Enrolling our kids full-time in daycare is what worked best for us!

Picking a daycare was so daunting. Living in Dallas, there are hundreds of options. We had to decide whether we wanted daycare to be closer to where we worked, or closer to our house. We chose closer to home, for convenience in the occasion we were off work and daycare was still open. Hello, long holiday break before kids live by the school district calendar!

We toured three daycares in total. One was closer to where I worked at the time. The other two were closer to home. Of the two closer to home, there was a $300 price difference. After touring the cheaper one and seeing them serve babies saltine crackers and sliced Velveeta cheese blocks for a snack, money didn't matter to me and I opted for the more expensive one.

They had fresh food! And it was organic! And they taught babies sign language, had an app for reports and pictures, and were open from 6:30 am to 6:30 pm.

And then we moved and found an even cheaper daycare than we toured previously. It was an older building with fewer kids, but the teachers were loving, and our kids were learning. (Literally, Brooklyn came home once when she was 2.5 years old and showed us pictures of the body and said, "this is the heart! It pumps the blood! These are blood vessels. They carry the blood." Talk about a jaw-dropper.) We realized all those extra perks at the 'primo' daycare weren't really doing anything for us except costing us more money. So, we opted out and we're still comfortable sending our kids to a cheaper, older location. The teachers were wonderful, and they truly cared for our children, and that is was really mattered most.

But remember, I said I wouldn't judge you for your choices, because ultimately you have to do what makes you feel comfortable. Your comfortability with where your child spends their day without you is really the most important.

I have to say, though. Daycare is a lifesaver. I often think about how much less developed my own children would be if it weren't for daycare. There are many moms who teach their children age-appropriate skills. And then there are moms who don't, like me. We rely on daycare to demonstrate life skills like drawing shapes and pooping in the toilet. When Brooklyn was 2.5, she could distinguish a pentagon from an octagon. How the hell did that happen?

Daycare did the brunt of the potty-training work, how to appropriately use a spoon, and learning numbers and colors. While we as parents are there to continue their education on the weekends, it starts with their teachers at daycare.

I do have guilt sometimes about not spending enough time with my children. I miss them so much during the day that it hurts sometimes. Working full-time and raising children isn't easy no matter how you do it. It feels weird to fully relinquish the care and safety of your baby to another person. But when you think about it, this is a natural progression anyway. As we get older, we spend more time out in the world than we do with our family at home. Our kids start kindergarten. And then they're in high school and in sports. And then they're in college and have jobs. It's normal and everyone does it. The guilt might resurface at times, but don't let yourself get absorbed in it.

And for those of you like me who feel bad, remember what spending time with your children is really like 90% of the time. The crying and diapers and spit up. It might be guilt-ridden at times, but some of us need that relief. Figure out what route of childcare is going to work best for you and your family's needs, and don't second guess it!

5 CARING FOR BABY

When it comes down to it, you can read all the books and take all the classes you want, but unless you've spent a large amount of your life taking care of babies, you might not really know anything about caring for a child. Reading about something is much different than being hands-on. But ya know what? I have complete faith in you. And this is why: they say that once you have kids, you have a new appreciation for your parents and the effort it took to raise you. But do you ever look at your parents, whether they're with a baby or not, and wonder how in the hell you're alive?

[Raises hand.]

If they can do it, you can do it. They were able to successfully bring you from infancy to adulthood without a baby monitor, fancy swaddles, organic formula or motorized swinging and singing contraptions. You turned out okay (I assume), and you have the benefit of having a baby in a world with a million amazing, albeit expensive, baby products to help you.

We already know there is a lot of work that goes into caring for a baby. Diapers need to be changed more often than you'd ever expect. Sleep. Ha! What is sleep?! And don't get me started on breastfeeding yet.

But do you know why caring for a baby—more specifically, a

newborn—is so difficult? It's because there is so little immediate reward. Your reward for a 2 AM round of changing a diaper, breastfeeding or bottle feeding, changing diaper again, pumping, then laying back in bed for maybe 30 minutes before it starts all over again is ear-piercing cries and wet shirts from milk leakage out of your boobs.

Don't get me wrong. I am not completely cold-hearted. Of course, they're cute, and newborn snuggles are kind of awesome. But the snuggles can get old real fast when it's the only way they will sleep, and they show zero signs of affection for you.

When I had Brooklyn, I discovered a distaste for the newborn and infant stage of her life. It is what I lovingly refer to as the Blob Stage. Eat, sleep, poop is their day job. And sometimes their night job. It's not until about 3 months that they'll perform a smile as a reaction to your face and not a bout of gas that just left their bellies. I thought for sure with Charlotte I would enjoy this newborn blob stage much more. I was totally wrong. It's so much better once babies will smile and play. And hold their own bottle. And sleep through the night.

Toddlers are hard in their own ways. There are temper tantrums. They become defiant little humans who demand ice in their water cup with a straw, along with the perfect mix of Goldfish and Cheerios in the 'regular' pink bowl that is actually the small bowl, not the regular-sized bowl. But you get to interact with toddlers, and they can be some of the funniest individuals on the planet. They begin to talk more and more each day. Seeing them bloom into their own little colorful personalities is fascinating. Toddlers might be ruthless at times, but babies are completely dependent on you with no way to express their feelings except their shrill cries.

Even though it's hard, a newborn isn't a newborn forever.

Eventually, you'll start to tell the difference between cries based on their volume or their body language. You might be able to recognize a hungry cry, which comes along with other hunger cues, like sucking on their fingers or on your arm when you pick them up. You'll also learn that sometimes their cries mean nothing other than 'pick me up and hold me,' and in that case, sometimes it is best to just let the cry go.

(Not all times, but sometimes, because mama needs some time to herself, too.)

Eventually, their cries will be more mature and not as jarring.

Eventually, they will sleep longer and longer. Their naps will be predictable, and a routine will start to take shape.

Eventually, they will look at you and play. You'll hear their first giggles and see them learn to roll and crawl.

The rewards of parenting eventually surface and remind you why you got knocked up in the first place.

You'll learn along the way that babies are resilient. You're probably going to do some things 'wrong.' You might accidentally cause them to cry. But aside from dropping them or shaking them or microwaving a bottle that is scalding hot inside—there isn't much you'll do that is going to cause them actual harm.

Isn't that a relief?

<u>Feeding Your Baby—Choosing a Food Source</u>

The only thing you really need to figure out how to do is to feed your baby. Honestly. All the other stuff is 'important,' but this is the number one thing that keeps your kid alive. That and cuddles and kisses from you because babies need to be loved. You're not going to have a problem with that, though. (Really. This is coming from a woman who wasn't even sure she wanted kids and was pretty sure her baby looked like an alien once it exited the vaginal canal. You'll be just fine.)

There are many options when it comes to feeding your child.

Breastfeeding only.
Combination of breastfeeding and bottle-feeding breastmilk.
Combination of breastfeeding and bottle-feeding formula.

Formula only.
Bottle-fed breastmilk only.

I want you to know that there is absolutely no WRONG way to feed your baby. The only wrong way is to not feed your baby, and I know we won't have to worry about that. Feeding your child can be a controversial topic, but only if you let others make it that way. You will hear 'breastfed is best.' But I want to tell you something different.

FED is best.

Breastfeeding is not an option for some women. And for others it is miserable, and therefore they choose it to not be their option. It wasn't my option. I tried with Brooklyn, and it lasted two weeks. I tried again with Charlotte and only made it a week before I stopped.

Breastfeeding was so painful for me. The first five days were okay, after which it took an immediate turn. The next few days I tried were so, so hard, even with a nipple shield. I had told myself I'd try again with our second baby, but only until I didn't want to anymore. I didn't last long. Both of my babies took to bottles incredibly well, fed much faster and seemed to eat more. It just made sense for us.

My experience is going to be vastly different from many others. There are many people who are of the opinion that breastfeeding is the best way to feed your child, and no other method compares. In my opinion, this is simply not true.

I also did not make my own baby food purees with Brooklyn, and only rarely with Charlotte. This surprised a lot of people, since I have a reputation of being a health nut. They assumed that I would want to spend the time chopping and boiling food, putting it into a food processor, then freezing it into blocks, and reallocating all those little frozen baby food blocks into something to store it in. Then, trying to figure out how to make and freeze so many different kinds of food so that my baby could get a variety of nutrients and not just sweet potatoes and bananas because they're the easiest to make.

Just reading that entire process makes my eye twitch a little.

There are plenty of options on the market for you to feel comfortable that your baby will get quality food in their bellies. For me, all the extra effort wasn't worth my time in making baby food. I already did so much food prep for my husband and myself, that buying purees from the grocery was so much easier in that season of life. If you want to make the time, that's great! I encourage you to do it. But if you'd rather spend your time doing something else, I support that decision as well.

We don't need to judge moms for what they're doing. We're all doing what works best for us so we can survive.

It's funny to me how very careful we are about feeding our babies. There is a loud emphasis on breastfeeding, Non-GMO formula, organic rice cereal and homemade purees so our babies can eat the best possible foods.

But you know what happens when your baby turns one? You buy them a ridiculously expensive smash cake that is loaded with sugar. You go to birthday parties where they eat chips and cupcakes. Your once vegetable-loving tiny human will turn her nose at roasted sweet potatoes—a food that used to be her favorite.

You might actually beg your child to eat a hamburger roll (without the hamburger) just so they have something in their stomach other than candy their grandma snuck past you.

So, what can you do? Will all be lost once your baby becomes a toddler? Not quite, but it won't always be easy. Like all things in life, do the best you can. Try to instill good habits. Lead by example. Yes, imagine that! If you want your kid to eat their vegetables, you need to be eating them, too. If your kid sees you eating chips and burgers for every meal, well, they will want to follow suit.

One tactic that has helped us get our toddler to eat her dinner is the 'no food after dinner' rule. It is really easy to let a toddler survive on snacks. Brooklyn is served her dinner, and she will eat until she tells us her belly is full. After that, no more food until breakfast. This will help her understand that we eat our dinner until we're full. It's also not an awful thing to teach what true hunger feels like. If I think she will be truly hungry because she ate two bites of pasta and one pea, then I'll set her dinner aside in anticipation she'll want more, and then she gets one more chance at a meal, but only of the food that we had for dinner. If she refuses her dinner food, especially when I know it is food she will usually eat, then she is probably not all that hungry. We also had to put a rule in place for her to ask to be excused from the dinner table. She got in the habit of taking a bite, getting up to play with a toy, then coming back for another bite…which is just another form of snacking.

Ultimately, feeding your child can be a total crapshoot. So, don't get yourself too hung up on what it is your child is eating. You can only do so much before your child has a decision-making mind of their own.

<u>Feeding Routines</u>

I wish, with all my heart, that I could tell you it will be easy to establish a feeding routine for your baby. The reality is, life can be vastly unpredictable in those newborn weeks and months. You can run with a general rule of feeding every 2 to 3 hours (or whatever your doctor suggests for you), but sometimes they'll require more frequent feedings. More rarely, they'll require less frequent feedings.

Around week 4 with Brooklyn and week 6 with Charlotte, I started feeding them at roughly the same times each day. It seemed like an eternity, but they had finally put themselves on a schedule that worked! And I mean that literally—they put themselves on a schedule. Not me. Those young babies are resistant to any type of schedule making you might try to impose. I tried harder with Charlotte, thinking more structured feeding would help her colicky nature, but there were times I'd think she should be hungry with her 2-hour bottle rotation, and she wouldn't touch it. Eventually, she had a very irregular eating pattern, ranging from 2 to 4 hours between bottles that I would have never predicted, but it worked for her.

There are other small routines you can build around feeding times. Oftentimes, our babies would fall asleep just after a feeding. To make sure I'd be able to lay them down, I changed their diaper before giving them a bottle. Once they were a couple of months old though, we started doing diaper change after feeding, for two reasons. One, the bottle started making them poop. Two, we tried to engage in a little bit of activity before laying down for a nap to help establish better sleep habits. We didn't want naps to be dependent on having had a feeding.

Another routine after a bottle is burping your baby. Typically, babies who are breastfed don't need to be burped, as they don't get the extra air during their feeding, which happens with a bottle. Burping is a routine that I legit did not know when I was a first-time mom. It's also something you would pick up on just watching other moms with babies, but I am unashamed to admit that I didn't burp Brooklyn after any of her bottles right away. As it turned out though, Brooklyn didn't really burp that much anyway. Charlotte, on the other hand, belched like a grown man at the local pub.

Hygiene

This whole baby hygiene section of the book just makes me giggle. There are so many things I never realized had to be done to keep a baby clean. I mean, babies just sit there and sleep. And you wipe their butt when they poop. How else could they possibly get dirty? Surely a quick bath now and then should cover it!

Ha!

Let me tell you about a thing I call 'neck cheese.' You see, when babies are born, they have no control of their neck. And as babies grow, they put on extra weight to keep them healthy. Since a baby's body is so little, all the extra fat just accumulates in rolls. And their cheeks get chubby. And it's just the cutest thing ever. But you know where else these little rolls accumulate? Around their neck. And basically, they don't have a neck because of these fat rolls—their oversized heads look directly attached to their teeny little bodies. Now, this would not be a problem at all if babies were efficient eaters. But they're learning, so we cut them some slack by providing them with bibs, wiping them clean, and staying calm while the breastmilk or formula dribble onto our clothes and furniture.

But do you know where else this milk or formula dribbles into? Their neck rolls. And if you aren't cleaning out their neck rolls with a wipe or washcloth in the bath almost daily, those little milk dribbles will sit there and form a gooey substance that smells like blue cheese.

I'm sorry if that makes you gag a little bit—it certainly made me gag the first time I discovered neck cheese on Brooklyn because I caught the smell of it before the sight of it—but it's a baby hygiene issue I never realized would exist. And it can be really easy to miss, especially if your baby has a hefty neck roll situation.

The rest of this section is a little more predictable, but we'll go through it one by one. If you're like me, it will be filled with things you didn't really think about.

Fingernails

What might almost be worse than fermented milk in the tiny crevices of your baby's body is cutting their teeny, tiny little daggers called fingernails. This is one of the hardest jobs on the planet, and I'd say this usually ends up on the mother's chore list. At least, my husband never attempted to cut our daughters' nails, which honestly is probably for the betterment of our whole family.

Baby fingernails are rubbery, which makes them really difficult to maintain. Sort of like stabbing a tiny ice cube with a butter knife that is sliding around on a plate—but at the same time your baby is holding that ice cube and you are frantically trying not to cut their little finger off. It's not far from the truth—you're holding a metal clipper next to your baby's skin and cutting a nail that is basically growing into said skin. Getting the clipper between the nailbed and the skin makes you want to sweat. Add flailing baby limbs on top of that, and the melty ice cube scenario makes sense.

Logic would tell you that a rubbery fingernail can't possibly also be described as a dagger. Though by the time you need to cut your baby's fingernails, you will have found out that babies have a tendency to define all sense of logic, so this is just another one of their magical qualities. In order to complete this task, you need to be a ninja.

Scenario one: pick them up and have someone distract them, while you quickly and expertly snap-through each finger to make the nails just short enough that you don't have a chance at nipping their skin but not long enough that daycare will send home notes that say 'Charlie is scratching herself, please cut her nails, ty.'

It's much more likely that before you feel comfortable with Scenario One, you are going to employ Scenario Two. In this technique, you wait for a time when your baby is sound asleep in a bouncer, jumper, car seat, etc. Then you quietly, with ninja-like skill, maneuver your way over and lift their hands ever so slightly that they don't awaken, and take your time clipping those daggers. I attempted this scenario once, but I forgot to wear my ninja suit. Brooklyn was asleep in her jumper—which is kind of hilarious and joyfully silent at the same time. I immediately regretted this attempt, wishing I had just left her alone and relished the silence. The first nail I cut was also nicked under the skin by the clippers, causing her thumb to bleed, which in turn caused her to awaken whilst yelling in pain. I'm even shaking my head at myself right now years later.

Nail cutting is a tricky little chore, so you should be prepared for it to be a little harder than you think. Or you could go with Scenario Three, which is really strange, so you may not want to go there. A friend once told me with her first baby, she bit off her baby's fingernails because she was too scared to cut them. As a mom, you'll probably go to your own desperate measures at one point or another so no judgment over here. Just a little bit of hesitation from me on this suggestion, is all.

Poop

I would say that nail-clipping is the worst of your baby hygiene problems, but honestly, you know the worst is going to be all the poop you have to deal with. Most of the time it's contained, so it's not a big deal aside from the fact it starts to smell once your baby is eating anything other than breastmilk. Poop can cause its own problems though. Like laundry. Oh lord, we could complain about the amount of laundry we would do for days. We're not gonna do that though. We're gonna keep talking about poop.

Fun fact! Did you know that babies can poop all the way up their back? It's another magical baby power, and it's called a blowout. It's also called a disgusting mess. Encountering more than one blowout in a day could mean your baby has diarrhea, or it could be a good indication that you need to go up to a bigger size in diapers. Diarrhea is more watery though, so you should be able to tell the difference. When a diaper is on too tight, either from poor application or a baby's bottom being too big for the diaper, it isn't loose enough to catch poop closer to the poop hole. When a baby poops, it is usually with force, and oftentimes when they're sitting or lying down. It doesn't take a physicist to understand that means poop has nowhere to go but up. Up, into the great beyond-the-diaper and into their cute little onesie I hope you didn't pay $25 for at a boutique.

So, now you have this baby that is literally covered in poop. And if you're lucky, no one else was holding your baby at the time of the blowout so they aren't covered in poop either. Changing your baby out of said 'poop onesie' takes some patience and precision. You could ask someone to help you navigate the situation, but I am not sure you'll get many volunteers. Depending on whether you have a changing table nearby that can withstand a good cleaning, you'll do one of two things. The first is to lay your baby on their back, lift their legs, remove the diaper, and slowly roll the onesie up so all of the poop is caught inside. It may then be safe to remove over their head. The second is to stretch the onesie out just enough so that you can pull it down over their body. This is usually what I'd do if the blow out was so bad, I had to undress baby while holding her on my tummy for fear of laying her down for a dirty version of a snow angel.

Of course, you could always put your baby in the sink and hose them down. But depending on your location and who was watching you do it, that might not be an option. And if you are cleaning up a blowout situation for your two-year-old that is soggy from the pool and blown all the way up their skin-tight, one-piece swimming suit, you're definitely going straight into the bathtub.

You'll quickly realize the importance of carrying extra baby clothes—and possibly even an extra shirt for yourself—in your diaper bag at all times. I quickly developed a distaste for onesies early on in motherhood for this very reason. Sleepers were the outfit of choice as long as they were socially appropriate, and then we switched to pants and shirts.

Diaper Rash

Poop not only causes parental angst when in the form of a blowout, but it can also cause diaper rash. When Brooklyn was a newborn, I didn't know what diaper rash looked like. I wasn't even aware that I should be looking for it. When I think about it, I also didn't realize babies needed to eat in the middle of the night, so quite obviously I had not set proper expectations for this whole motherhood thing very well.

Brooklyn was two weeks old when Kyle's parents came to visit. During the first diaper change his mother did for me, she noticed a bit of diaper rash and applied some cream. I felt kind of embarrassed at first, thinking I should have noticed that. I mean, I did notice that it was a little red between her cheeks, but I didn't realize that was diaper rash. It seemed like it should be more severe to warrant the application of diaper cream. In reality, a little bit of redness can cause irritation. And there isn't any harm in putting on diaper cream, so if you're unsure, just go for it! Better safe than sorry on that one. Both our girls had diaper rash so bad at times it had broken skin and required a prescription diaper cream. These cases were both caused by a bad case of diarrhea. I wouldn't say diaper rash that bad is always normal, but if you're not able to clear it up or it keeps getting worse, a call to your pediatrician might be a good idea.

Cradle Cap

The first observation of cradle cap may be confusing. Even if you've heard of it but never seen it, you might just think your baby has a fungus growing on his scalp. Or question whether or not you forgot to wash their hair for their entire life.

Cradle cap is a yellow or grayish-brown scaly substance that sticks to the top of a baby's scalp. It looks really gross and can be hard to remove. And if you feel slightly OCD at times, you're going to be fighting the urge to pick at it. You aren't supposed to do this though because picking at it can irritate your baby's head. Cradle cap itself doesn't cause irritation, so there's no need to add potential itching or soreness to the situation of our own accord. A quick Google search will tell you it is either the cause of excessive oil production or a fungal infection. Please do not freak out about this (remember, you shouldn't be googling things anyway). Cradle cap is common and will either go away by itself, or you can purchase a shampoo to help get rid of it. And if you notice it and are concerned, once again, give that pediatrician of yours a call.

Both my daughters had it. Brooklyn's took a while to go away. Charlotte's probably would have gone away faster if I gave her a bath more often so I could wash her hair.

But ya know, second kid problems.

Bath Time

Speaking of bath time…don't beat yourself up if you only manage to bathe your children once a week. It happens more often than I probably should admit, but my kids are lucky to be bathed twice in one week. I will say as Brooklyn got older, we got more diligent—and that's only because wiping her own butt after she pooped was a skill she slowly developed. Any time you change your kid into pajamas and have to wonder 'What's that smell?' it's probably time to up your bath time frequency.

That said, bath time is necessary because even though babies don't play in the dirt like toddlers, they do get dirty. Please recall the neck cheese scenario. Also, if your baby is like mine were, then there will be the cutest little fat rolls for days on all their extremities. Those little rolls need the fuzz and slobber cleaned out from time to time!

Now, we have established that bath time is necessary. We have yet to establish that bath time is enjoyable.

Not all babies enjoy bath time. Brooklyn screamed bloody murder while getting bathed the first two months of her life. It actually took an entire month for me to get the courage to try to bathe her—my husband dutifully took on that chore until I was ready. Luckily, there are several types of baby tubs on the market now that can make this easier. We used one made of foam, that was like a wedge that folded in half and fit crossways in the kitchen sink. With Brooklyn, we were able to easily move right into an inflatable tub because she was able to sit when she was 6 months old. Charlotte proved more challenging because she outgrew the kitchen sink tub before she was able to sit, so I basically had to hold her up in the inflatable tub the entire time. The only thing harder than dressing a baby with flailing limbs is bathing a baby you have to hold in the tub with flailing limbs. Needless to say, her bath time duration was short.

Brooklyn started to love the bath around 8 months. She started hating getting her hair wet around 2 years old. It was uber frustrating, especially because her hair had gotten long enough to get in her face while she was eating. Her hair was nearly always covered in food to some extent, so skipping the hair wash step was not an option. In hindsight, I suppose I could be grateful to Brooklyn's aunt who sent her a bag of 50+ rubber duckies for Valentine's Day. They served as a decent distraction during the shampoo massage and rinse.

It's weird that I sometimes forget I should clean my little humans the same as I would clean myself (a mostly normal human). You need to keep them clean in all the same places. A couple of places to remember are all the little extra hiding places in your baby girl's lady parts, behind their ears, and also in their ears. I once discovered a half-inch long tube of wax folded up inside Brooklyn's ear at her two-month pediatric check-up because I had not spent any time cleaning her ears. Major face to the palm. Make sure you keep those safety swabs on hand to do a quick check right after bath time is over!

<u>Strength Building</u>

I sometimes imagine what it would be like to have nearly every activity you do be a form of strength building. For babies, bottles are too heavy, waving a rattle is a muscle endurance workout, and raising their head for more than two seconds is nearly impossible. Babies get tired easily and sleep a lot because all these things wear them out so much.

And then I wonder, do babies get sore like adults do? If they do tummy time too long, does their neck hurt? Or do they cry long before they get to that point? Either way, it's no wonder that babies cry a lot. Everything is difficult until they learn new skills.

When I was home on maternity leave, I had no idea whether or not I was engaging my baby in the proper skill-building activities. How much 'tummy time' was enough? How many times a day? When should I give her toys?

As it turns out, there isn't a lot of thought that needs to go into this. You're going to naturally do things that will allow your baby to build strength, like laying her on your chest. She might try to look up at you, and that's the same thing as tummy time. You might lay them on their back on the floor, so you can go grab a water from the kitchen, and you come back and BAM—she's on her belly. Rolling over is strength building, too. Gotta kick those little legs!

One thing to note would be that you should not always lay your baby in the same exact spot. When Brooklyn was two weeks old, we discovered that she napped really well in her Mamaroo when she was propped up on her side a little bit. So, we carefully stuck a blanket behind her back, so she was tilted just a little bit. She was always monitored so that she didn't somehow roll over onto her face. We continued this for the next six weeks, propping her up on the same side—multiple times a day, for as long as she would nap. Her two-month check-up came around, and Doc told us her head was getting flat on one side.

I felt like an idiot. But really, why would I have ever thought I'd be molding my baby's head flat?

After a month of propping her up on the other side, her head rounded out and she was just fine!

<u>Baby's Milestones</u>

Watching a baby's milestones might be the most exciting thing you can do as a parent. That could possibly be a vastly invalid statement, but when you're huddled over your six-month-old spouting words of encouragement to roll over, it feels pretty damn exciting. It's also funny when you look back on it—cheering for a baby as she frantically kicks her leg over so she can get up onto her perfectly round belly. Unsure of whether it'll end in a smile, because she can push herself up on her elbows, or if she will cry because she face planted hard into the rug.

It makes you feel proud as a parent when your baby can do something new. Your baby can do the things that babies are 'supposed' to do! Whew! You can scratch off some of those minor developmental challenges off your 'to-worry' list. Because worry might be a trap you get sucked into when it comes to your baby's milestones.

Why? Because some other baby at daycare might have started rolling over at 4 months old when your baby struggled to enjoy tummy time for more than 30 seconds at 5 months old. And your baby's older sister might have been an early roller—even an early crawler—while your husband lovingly referred to your second baby as 'lazy' because she just wants to hang out on her back.

If it sounds like I am speaking from experience, you would be correct. Rolling over is a developmental milestone the pediatrician might start asking about at 4 months. Charlotte showed no sign of it that early and only started rolling over with some ease a week or two after she turned 6 months. Did I worry? A little. But not a lot because I learned with my first daughter that a baby gets to his or her milestones on their own time. And just like anything else in life, comparison is an ugly thing.

Just because your baby doesn't crawl, walk, talk, or potty train as quickly as another baby doesn't mean anything is wrong! It is natural for parents to worry but comparing a milestone to another baby will only make you feel poorly. Chances are you pediatrician will shrug it off or suggest activities for your baby, and if there is really a problem, they will bring it to your attention at an appropriate time.

Instead of wanting your baby to chug along to the next new thing, try to enjoy the stage they're in. I can't believe those words were just written by my fingertips, because it's a more sentimental concept than I will typically humor. But it is true that you will look back in loving memory of the 'baby phase' and want to experience it again just for a little while. (That's what other people's babies are for!)

It's okay for your baby to be off-schedule in milestones compared to any other baby. Do you know what else is okay? Not wanting them to start some of those milestones for less sentimental reasons.

Once a baby starts moving, that baby does not want to stop. Even learning new skills as small as kicking their legs up to grab their feet— it doesn't stop, and it makes changing a diaper a lot more difficult. Thrusting their legs in the air to play with their toes is a never-ending activity. Do you know what else doesn't stop once it starts? Crawling. Gone will be the days when you can set your baby on the floor and then go do the dishes with her out of sight for a few minutes as she plays with a rattle. Say hello to baby proofing, running around the house after a speed-crawling child, and a fun new game called 'Where's Charlie?!'

I've heard stories about second or third babies crawling and walking early. Way early. Way too early for you to be ready for it, depending on the age difference between siblings. I even heard once about a mom who had four babies, and the last one, her only son, started walking way before he was one. She would push him down on the ground when he got up to keep it from happening too soon.

Okay, so it was my mom who told that story about my brother, and maybe no one else is ever going to hear a story like that. But you might hear a mom joke about that because the feeling is certainly there. Once a baby can crawl or walk, it is a total game-changer.

I have to say, though, the traditional milestones of rolling over, crawling, walking and potty training were not necessarily the best. Alright, so potty training was probably the ultimate best once it was done, although getting there is a beast. But there are so many other milestones that aren't celebrated enough.

Your first five-hour sleep

Getting your baby to sleep through the night is the ultimate milestone and one that is worth popping champagne over. But your first five-hour sleep? Arguably, just as good. That means you're likely only getting up once at night! Once is doable for a longer term without ripping your hair out. Once is also going to happen semi-frequently even after your baby is sleeping through the night. It will take some time for them to consistently sleep 10-12 hours, and you can confidently assume you'll get a full night of sleep.

Like all things, every baby is different here, but there are certainly resources you can find to help you learn sleep cues and how to sleep train your baby. If you do not feel confident in sleep training your baby on your own, I highly recommend you seek advice!

Holding a bottle

If Kyle and I had to do one of those 'who knows each other better' games where you both write each other's answer to a question on a dry erase board, I am 89% sure we'd both write 'holding their own bottle' as our favorite baby milestone. The first time Brooklyn was strong enough to feed herself, we looked at each other and rejoiced. It was a true present from God—the answer to a test of patience. You might read that sarcastically, but it is sort of not sarcastic.

When you and your significant other both have to get ready in the morning and commute to work, the constant attention required for an infant throws your entire routine out of whack. I mean, you just had a baby, so everything is different now anyway. You're welcome for stating the obvious. But going back to work after a couple of months or so can be stressful enough without figuring out how to do all the things you need to do before you actually sit down at your desk.

This is the scenario that went through my head most mornings when we had Brooklyn. It took a solid month after I was back at work before we had a routine figured out.

How will I work out now? I'd have to get up at 4 am. Will I have enough time to dry my hair if I shower? Baby's awake. Diaper change! Can't forget to dress the baby now; she probably shouldn't wear pajamas all day at school. Can someone please come dress me so I don't have to decide what to wear? Time to feed the baby! Diaper change! Maybe feed myself? Nah, fasting is a thing now. Oh, gotta prep all the bottles and diaper bag! Where's her blanket? Where's my workbag? Where's my phone? Can you strap her into the car seat? Where's my sanity?

Layer on whether or not you're sleeping well yet on top of that, and you can easily have a chaotic situation on your hands. Sure, it can get a little easier if you know what you're in for every morning. But it doesn't necessarily make it less chaotic. There is a real reason that families with babies are late anywhere they go.

But once your baby can feed herself a bottle? It literally feels like you're living under a rainbow. It frees up 10-20 minutes of time. Do you know how much you can get done in 10-20 minutes? A lot. You can pack all the baby stuff, all your stuff, and maybe even pack a healthy lunch in that amount of time. So, when your baby can hold their bottle, praise Jesus, because it's a miracle.

Drinking real milk

Maybe your baby has a dairy allergy, so you won't transition to actual cow's milk, but you'll eventually transition to a different type of milk other than breastmilk or formula. If you breastfed your child up until this point, then you didn't experience the costly alternative that is formula. While I don't regret my choices to not breastfeed and strictly use formula after 1-2 weeks, I do reserve my right to still complain about the cost of formula.

But there comes a point when you get to cut off formula altogether. Cold turkey. This celebratory milestone is usually overshadowed by baby's first birthday, which coincides with this milestone but is of seemingly equal in importance. I do stand in my belief that the milk switch doesn't get near the credit as a milestone that it deserves.

Starting real food for baby, in general, is going to keep money in your bank account. Food purees, even if you buy them instead of making them yourself, cost less than formula. Although they add a certain time and mess factor, saving money is worth the tradeoff.

Once a baby drinks real milk, he is no longer a baby anymore, but a toddler. It might be surprising how much less liquid it seems your toddler actually drinks. It makes sense though. As a baby, bottles are their only form of nutrition. But a toddler eats real food, which is more caloric. Their bodies are still quite small, so they don't need a drastically increased level of fluid intake to survive. Some adults barely touch water in a day, and your toddler has his own willful decision-making capabilities now, so don't worry too much about how much they are drinking.

It's easy enough to let them carry a water cup around wherever they go. Don't do that with a milk cup though. It might get lost and that's not a smell you want in your home.

Eating table food

No more food purees! No more spoon-feeding! As I should have anticipated, both my daughters began to enjoy table food at very different ages, but both provided me with another sliver of freedom.

It took some time before our babies would eat whatever else we were having for dinner, but I'd typically have some separate ingredients on hand that would work. I'm not going to make any recommendations on foods you should feed your child. Your doctor will be able to provide you with age-appropriate food selections, along with the size of the food you should be offering. You may also want to ask your doctor about the appropriate way to feed your children the top allergen foods as well.

Your first full night of sleep

This is the second sleep-related milestone, and that is because sleep is the best thing for both baby and baby's parents. I believe it is also the root cause of most frustration as it relates to parenting a newborn. Small irritabilities are amplified when one is operating on little sleep.

There will be two distinct emotions you'll experience on the morning after your first full night of sleep.

Emotion One: Fear. You will believe there is no way humanly possible that your child slept completely through the night. You will check the monitor to inspect for breathing, and you will then run up to your child's room to double confirm they are still breathing. You will find that your baby is indeed still breathing.

Emotion Two: Euphoria. It is true. You slept through the night! It is also possible that it will happen again, and that uninterrupted sleep is just within your reach.

While this may feel like Christmas morning, I would encourage you not to get too cozy in jammies the next night. Sleeping through the night for the first time is incredible progress, and certainly should be celebrated. But we must be realistic and drop the expectations that this will be the new norm. It is easy to get trapped in the expectation that once means always, and then be disappointed when it doesn't happen consecutively.

The important thing is that it did happen once, and that means it can happen again. And the end will be near, but possibly after a regression or two. For now, enjoy the full nights you do get, but continue to keep your coffee maker set to brew at 5 am each day.

Forward-facing car seat

Depending on the type of vehicle you drive, this may not be a big deal. But I currently drive a smallish Ford Fusion with two car seats in the back, and I have a husband that is 6' 2", so it's kind of a big deal for us.

You see, rear-facing car seats—whilst entirely necessary for your child's safety—take up a lot of room in a back seat. The spacious demand of a rear-facing carrier and base means that the front seats can only slide back as far as the car seat will allow. If you're 5'5" like me, it isn't a big deal. But if you are tall, it means your vehicle is not going to be comfortable to ride in one of the two seats.

Probably not a big deal for most people. I will argue that tall people have vehicles that accommodate their tall bodies. Or maybe you have a family like mine, where you drive a suitable car that is paid off, and your husband drives a gas-guzzling monster truck. The car seats are the only real argument my husband ever has as to why we need an upgrade, but I just can't justify having a car payment, even if my car is less of a vehicle and more of an ultra-powerful stroller.

Once you move from rear-facing to forward-facing car seats, most of the spatial dynamic issues are resolved. Although sometimes that means your child only has a couple of inches between a seat and where her feet hang but ultimately that means there is no room for kicking, which is actually a hidden bonus of tall-husband syndrome.

Forward-facing car seats are also easier to physically get a child in the seat. Your child can try to climb into it like a sloth in a tropical rainforest, or you can propel their bottom into the seat without too much effort. Eventually, they can climb out of a seat pretty easily as well, giving you time to unload work bags or groceries before they make it inside the house. It's a great distraction for a few minutes!

By this time, you will learn that distraction is key, and a skill you'll continue to sharpen the rest of your toddler-mom life.

Self-play

There are two stages of self-play. The first is a true self-play, for example, when your baby starts to engage with toys and play on the rug in front of you while you get to enjoy your morning coffee without too many interruptions. Neither of my children found happiness in a motion-inhibited state, which leads me to suggest that you are likely to reach this stage once your baby can crawl around a little bit.

The second kind of self-play will happen much later, maybe sometime before two years. They start to 'sing' songs, dance around and babble to themselves while looking at a book. They might make funny faces or go through a sequence of animal noises (Brooklyn's lion roar was on point). This is a fun self-play, not only for them but for you. It takes a little less effort, and it will probably make you laugh hysterically.

<u>Diaper Bag Essentials</u>

Now that you'll be bringing a baby with you most place you go, you'll need to pack and carry a diaper bag. We already covered diaper bag recommendations under The Registry, but now we're going to talk about what you should actually put in it. It can be really easy to load it with too much stuff, making it really heavy. We're already carrying around a baby (plus the car seat in many scenarios), so having a diaper bag that won't weigh you down is even more important! Also, you might not have the best posture these days if you're hunched over a baby while breastfeeding, so we want to make sure you're comfortable. (Did you just sit up straight? I did too.)

These are some essentials you'll want to make sure you have with you when you're out and about with baby:

- Diapers: Generally, I'd pack 1 diaper for every 2 hours we would be gone, plus 1 extra because unexpected poops happen!
- Wipes: Try a travel-size pack of wipes, or a container you can stick a large chunk of wipe in. Large zip-lock bags work well if you don't want to buy something extra. I wouldn't travel with a full pack of wipes, because they're really heavy.
- Change of clothes: For baby, not you. Although an extra shirt for you could probably come in handy sometimes, too!
- Diaper cream: Try putting some from a larger container into a small container, to eliminate extra weight.
- Hand sanitizer: Not all diaper changes happen in convenient locations like a bathroom.
- Tri-fold changing pad: For those diaper changes in an inconvenient location.
- Bags to store dirty diapers: There are baby-specific bags you can buy for these. But zip lock bags or even plastic grocery

bags work just as well.
- Supplies for feeding: breastfeeding cover, bottles, formula, etc.

<u>Tips for Traveling with Baby</u>

Just like anything you do with baby, flying (or traveling in general) can be overwhelming. Brooklyn had four round-trip flights under her belt by the time she was four months old, so we learned a lot about traveling with baby really quickly! We were very blessed that she traveled well each flight. Babies still sleep a lot before they are four months old, so that certainly helped. Believe me, though, we got many side-eye stares from people as we boarded each flight, and people sighed with relief as we walked by their aisles. I will say, after traveling with a child, I will forever give grace and say prayers for other parents who do the same. There are just some situations when you cannot control what your children will do, and flying is one of them.

There are some things that can help you feel less stressed and miserable while trapped in a 2x2 foot box with your baby. The first thing starts with booking your flights. Try to time the flights as best as possible with feeding and naptimes. If you can feed your baby towards the end of flight boarding and during takeoff, this will help with any pressure in their ears and get them sleepy for the rest of the flight. This was a tried and true method for us on most of our flights with Brooklyn.

Baby wearing is also very helpful! It's nice to have the stroller while you are in the airport but try putting your baby in a wrap or carrier as you board the plane, or after you have finished feeding. Being close to mom (or dad!) will help them be comfortable and warm, and again help to get them cozy and gear up for a good long nap. There were several flights when I wore Brooklyn in a carrier the entire time as she slept.

Bottle feeding can also be tricky if you suddenly need a bottle mid-flight. Bring an empty coffee thermos with you through security. Once you are through, go to a coffee shop or restaurant and ask them to fill it with hot water. This tip is great for babies who don't like to drink formula at room temperature (mine did not). It keeps you from having to find a microwave or hot water to heat up a bottle if you're in an inconvenient spot. The water is usually really hot, so have an extra bottle of water handy to mix it with and adjust the temperature if needed. We did this when we are out running errands or would be driving in the car for a long period of time. Heating water above its drinking temp helps so that it doesn't get too cold for baby to drink. Also, find some containers that will hold your pre-portioned formula. Some bottle companies make inserts for their bottles that will hold the formula. We used smaller plastic containers we already had. Either way, portioning out a few more of these than you need is helpful in case something gets spilled, dropped, or your baby is hungrier than you expected.

Help! My Baby Won't Calm Down

It's going to happen, and it is going to be frustrating. I was naïve when we had Brooklyn. My minimal knowledge about how a baby operated led me to extreme defeat at times with motherhood. You probably know that babies are supposed to 'eat, sleep, and poop.'

What people fail to make clear is the fourth activity on a baby's list. It's actually 'eat, sleep, poop and cry.' Or more accurately, 'eat, cry, sleep, cry, poop, cry.'

Yes, all babies will cry. And some will cry softer than others, or more often than others. But not all people are wired mentally or emotionally to handle a crying baby—especially when it seems there is no way to soothe them.

Every person has a threshold of what they can handle. There are moms who have three kids that often all cry at once, but they're somehow able to block it out and keep going, knowing that it is just what kids do and there's nothing to prevent them from crying. Your reaction to how your children cry will be a learning experience for them. If you pick them up every time they peep, or give in every time they want a snack, they'll learn that's what will happen. So, it may also be a learning experience for you. A practice in patience.

While one mom's cry meter might have a higher roof than others, I can tell you one thing for certain. Mine is not very high. And neither is my husband's.

Nearly everyone who knew anything about babies made comments about Brooklyn being an easy baby. I literally remember thinking, "If this is easy, then I don't want to experience hard." (Lucky for me, I did get to experience hard when Charlotte erupted from the canal two-and-a-half years later.) But even with Brooklyn's supposedly easy-going gracefulness, there were plenty of times when it was damn near impossible to get her to calm down.

The 'witching hour' were two words I hadn't heard without a reference to Halloween until Brooklyn was just over a month old. We were at a friend's place for dinner. Our social life resumed to semi-normal fashion once she was on a schedule because we craved social settings, and I wasn't napping during the day anyhow. But it seemed that every evening around 6 pm, no matter where we were, and whether we had access to all the swings and bouncers and pacifiers, Brooklyn would be fussy for about an hour or so. In my obvious distress for lack of ability to calm her down, my friend said to me, 'Oh, this must be her witching hour.'

Say what? What the hell is a witching hour? And why does it so accurately describe this sweet-turned-monster child?

Turns out, this is something many babies and their parents experience, and it is quite normal. Like most things with children, there is just speculation as to why this mysterious hour or two of our life must exist every day, but it could be a range or combination of changes in hormones in breastmilk-fed babies to overstimulation from a day's worth of activities. Babies eventually outgrow it, and with time will get better at soothing themselves when they are worked up.

It's important to know, though, that this is likely going to happen, and your inability to calm them down says absolutely nothing about you as a parent.

The witching hour isn't the only instance when a baby won't calm down. I'm sure you've heard about 'colicky babies,' and you also might not understand what that means. Colic is not an actual 'condition' of babies. It is more of a catch-all term when a baby just cries most of the time. There doesn't always seem to be a reason, but your pediatrician will work with you to try and understand what might be causing it. The internet will tell you that many times colic is the result of a digestive issue. That was, in fact, the case when we experienced colic with Charlotte. But there is no actual research around it, leaving colic to be another grueling mystery of having a child.

Having a support system in place is more important than ever when you're going through any period of time with an inconsolable baby. Lean on your spouse, friends, and family for support, even if it is to vent about how hard it is to deal with a baby you can't calm down. Just because these things are normal doesn't mean they are any less difficult. And it doesn't mean you aren't doing your job as a parent, either! I remember feeling like I didn't want to complain to my friends about having a crying baby. But in the end, women who have experienced it will be there for you. They will listen and empathize because they know it is hard.

If it seems like your baby is crying non-stop, you might have people tell you she has colic. I talk about our experience with a colicky baby in a couple of chapters, but it is best addressed with your pediatrician. All colic-related experiences that I know had some kind of issue concerning their digestive system, however, this is not always believed to be or seems to be the cause. A quick Google search will give you lots of statistics on colic and can reassure you that most babies with colic are not in pain. Although we know we shouldn't be Googling at all. If you are experiencing what you believe to be colic, be sure to address it with your pediatrician.

Most babies do not have colic. But all babies will cry at some point, and you won't know how to calm them down. It is hard to remember that crying is the only way a baby can express they are uncomfortable or want something. Crying is their only form of communication. When this happens, try to run through this list of things to see if something might be bothering them!

These are the standard three things most people recommend or tell you to try if a baby is crying:

- Feeding them
- Check for a wet or dirty diaper
- Rock to sleep because they need a nap (if only it were THAT easy)

There are so many other reasons that could cause a baby to cry. Think about things that might make you feel uncomfortable or cause you to get up from where you are sitting and make a change in your environment.

- Too hot: remove some clothes or a blanket
- Too cold: provide a blanket
- Needs to change position: sit up or lay down, move arms around, prop on their side
- Needs to change position again: if you don't get it right the first time
- Bright lights: try to turn off a light or draw a curtain
- Something scared her: I once saw a meme about babies crying, and one of the reasons was that mom farted and it scared the baby. While I'm certainly not going to accuse you of having gas, something weird like this could be a possibility!
- Wants a blanket: even if baby isn't cold, sometimes a blanket can be soothing

Some solutions above might work, but you can also try these soothing techniques:

- Patting their bottom
- Rubbing their back
- Sh sounds
- Other white noise
- Switching the type of baby seat that they're in, i.e., Swing vs bouncer

<u>Use of Technology</u>

Just like the various number of brands that exist for baby-related items, there are lots of different apps you can download to help track routines with a baby. Some are more helpful than others, with age-appropriate tips and suggestions for care. But I'm going to advise you not to use apps at all.

I'm a numbers person, so I fell into this trap. I started tracking how long I was breastfeeding on each side, how many wet or dirty diapers Brooklyn had, and how long she slept. My thought process was that I could recognize patterns that would show me a routine (unfortunately, no apps on the market actually help with that, as none of your input is ever analyzed together). However, all it did was make me feel like I wasn't doing enough. If she didn't feed as long one day as she did the previous day, I assumed something was wrong.

Instead of using apps, I suggest you keep two phone numbers ready:
1. A mom you trust to give you a realistic answer to your question (maybe that's your mom or a close friend)
2. Your pediatrician

Don't be afraid to call your pediatrician with weird questions or concerns. They have nurses on staff who will talk through your concerns and give you actual advice on when you should be concerned about something. It might also help you rationalize whether your concern is warranted. If you'd call your mom about it, but your gut says you don't need to call your pediatrician, then chances are everything is just fine.

Instead of using an app, I went old-fashioned notetaking in my iPhone and wrote down what boob was used to feed my baby last (which didn't last long as I switched to bottles pretty early), and what time the feed started. That's it.

Spending your time in apps can be just as bad as spending it online searching WebMD for an obscure symptom you think your baby has. It gets you down the rabbit hole of doom, and you don't need to do that to yourself.

6 THE BIRTH AND THE HOSPITAL STAY

Your birth experience will be so different from any other woman's. It's hard to really prepare for it. Whether you have a natural vaginal birth, c-section or induction, each pregnancy is a different case. Some women require a specific birthing plan, and other choose it. You might not want an epidural, but you end up choosing one. You might not want to be induced, but you might need to be. There is so much unknown in the birth of a child, and that's what makes it so scary. The only thing I can do is tell you about my own experience.

I was straight-up terrified to give birth to my first child.

My doctor even kinda made fun of me (don't worry, we have a very sarcastic relationship). I told him that I was scared because I don't really do well with hospitals and blood, and it was hard for me to even get the required blood draws at my check-ups. He just looked at me and said, 'Well, you probably should have thought of that before you got pregnant.'

The truth is, I think that giving birth was what kept me from thinking I wanted to have kids in the first place. The whole thing sounds miserable. But women have been doing this forever. Even before drugs were invented. Talk about 'female power,' having enough strength to willingly let another human rip your vagina open. There ain't no man on the planet, dead or alive, who'd have agreed to that.

In my frightened 37-week pregnant state, I naturally did the bravest thing possible and begged my doctor to induce me at that week's check-up. I then learned that legally you cannot be induced before 39-weeks without a necessary medical circumstance. At least, I assume it was legal, he just said that he could absolutely not, and that being 'miserable in pregnancy' did not qualify for early induction. (Don't gawk, I know that the baby still needs that time for development, too, I am not a total monster. I just desperately wanted to be done.)

So, I waited in fear—and in anticipation—that I might go into labor at any moment. I am not going to report an actual statistic on this because it really doesn't matter, but the majority of first-time pregnancies go right up until or past the due date. That was another piece of news cutely delivered to me at my 37-week appointment.

You know, the last thing I wanted to hear.

But at 39-weeks on Tuesday, April 26, 2016, after getting my belly measured and a vaginal exam to check dilation, my doctor helped me sit up and said, 'Wanna have a baby on Friday?' I am not lying or ashamed when I say I was equally as happy (or happier) on that day as I was the day Brooklyn was born. I was thrilled for the first time since I peed on a stick 9 months before.

He then offered me what he called the 'Princess Package,' where I'd come in early in the morning, get an IV drip for Pitocin, then get my epidural as soon as I wanted. Like, right away. While I consider myself more of a queen than a princess, this sounded like the most optimal way to push a child out of my body. I accepted his offer.

I chose to be induced for both of my pregnancies. Many women would never choose to go this route for their own reasons, and that is completely okay. When the time comes, you might not feel comfortable giving your baby an eviction notice. It is okay to give birth when, where and how you (and your doctor or midwife, I suppose) choose to do it. I had a friend talk about wanting to have a drug-free, natural birth because she just wanted to see what the contractions felt like. The way she said it made me feel a little inferior for opting out of that route. May I also add, that this friend hadn't been pregnant yet, nor was she actively trying to have children. The thing about a drug-free, natural birth? That is not for me. It may or may not be for you. I knew that no matter how I gave birth, I wouldn't let myself feel like any less of a woman compared to the next because I didn't feel as much pain.

Elective inductions do have their own risks, just like a natural birth or a c-section might. Your doctor will cover all of those for you, to be sure you'll make an informed decision. The other thing about elective inductions is that they are not 100% guaranteed. Even in a big hospital in Dallas, TX, there was a chance for us to get bumped off the schedule. You have to wait for a call in the evening before you go in to confirm. This is because the hospital needs to make sure they have enough room for any medically necessary inductions the next day.

I was more anxious waiting for that call with Brooklyn than I was about the induction process itself. I tried to remind myself there was a chance it might not happen, but I was so committed to the idea of having her the next day. The call came with positive news, and I was told not to eat anything after midnight and to show up at the hospital the next morning at 8 AM.

There's something weird about knowing it's your last night as a family of two. Kyle and I went out to a nice dinner that night, and then we came home to watch TV. It felt relatively normal, but it was more silent than usual. You can't be fully prepared for what's about to happen to your life when you have a baby. I don't remember how well I slept that night, but if I had to guess, it was not great.

We woke up early the next morning to make sure everything I needed was packed, the car seat was installed, and Kyle had his electronics properly charged. The induction process can vary depending on how well your body is ready for it, so we brought our Roku to plug in to the TV so we could watch Scandal (bringing you back to 2016 right there). True Princess Package in action.

Being early in the morning, there was no traffic on our drive to the hospital, so we got there about 15 minutes early. We parked, and Kyle reached to turn up the radio to wait out a few minutes, assuming we wouldn't get placed into our room right away since we were early.

Then I started bawling. The weight of the unknown that I'd been carrying the last 9 months melted and poured through my eyeballs. I was about to walk into one of my biggest fears, with no option of turning back. We sat in the truck for a few more minutes, then I cleaned up my face enough to not look like total emotional wreckage, and we walked inside.

I had pre-registered with the hospital as instructed by my doctor, so the whole check-in process was easy, especially since I was not checking in under the duress of labor.

Going to a room to 'check-in' to have your baby is also weird. You go in as two people, and later that day, you know you're leaving as three. And being induced, it's a lot of waiting for the family of three part.

Once we got in our room, I was instructed to change into my gown and wait for the nurse. There are a few ways to be induced, but I was given Pitocin via an IV drip. I also had to have an antibiotic because I tested positive for group B strep (GBS). You'll get tested for this once your doctor starts vaginal exams during your last month of check-ups. Most women don't test positive for it, and you can test positive for it for one pregnancy but not another. You can ask your doctor about GBS, but they'll have in your medical charts that you need an antibiotic once you're in labor to prevent passing it to the baby, and you'll both be just fine.

The nurse came after some time and started to get me prepped for my IV port. The thing you might not know about me is that I do not like needles. Needles and I have never gotten along. I once fainted at the vet's office when my dog got a vaccine, so I had a lot of fear to overcome with this whole pregnancy thing. But here I was, so fearful about finally getting that epidural that's supposed to be this 'big huge needle'…that it took my poor nurse almost thirty minutes to even get my little IV put in right. Literally. I'd had probably 10 blood draws throughout pregnancy, and this was really nothing different, but I had myself in such a tizzy. I nearly passed out twice, Kyle had to hold a barf bag in front of me, and I had to do some breathing exercises. The nurse said, 'Honey, if you're this worked up over the needle, it's gonna be a really long day!'

I must have needed to get the whole frantic fainting thing out of my system because I never reached that point the rest of the day. (Not that it's a thing that usually happens when you're giving birth unless you're like me and even the smell of a hospital makes your vision go fuzzy.)

Even getting the epidural wasn't that bad. There was no chance in hell that I wasn't getting one. While I wouldn't say I take drugs for just anything, this was something I knew I wouldn't skip out on. For me, needing to feel that pain, or taking the chance that somehow my baby would come so fast that I wouldn't have an option to get an epidural wasn't worth it. (That does happen, by the way. Getting an epidural itself doesn't necessarily take a lot of time, but it does take roughly a half hour to get one ordered and have the anesthesiologist get to you. Sometimes there just isn't time, if the baby is coming fast enough!)

The reason the epidural wasn't that big a deal for me is because I didn't see it. I have no idea how big the actual needle was that he used, or what the process looked like, and I am never going to Google it either. That said, it would probably be difficult to get one placed when you're in the middle of fast or hard contractions. To get the epidural, you lean on the edge of the hospital bed and curl your back up, bending forward with a pillow in front of you to be comfortable. They swipe your lower back with iodine to clean it, which is really cold. Then all you feel is pressure. It sort of feels like when you need to crack your back, but you can't—though it's a little more intense than that. It's not pain, just pressure. The result is a tiny little tube inside your lower back you'll have to keep track of throughout the day so it doesn't rip out, which can't really happen because you won't be able to move or walk. The tube is also taped to your back to secure it.

And then, it's done! Done with the epidural anyway.

After the epidural is in, it's just a long waiting game. Brooklyn wasn't born for another 8 hours after I got my epidural, and Charlotte was another 7. This is where you need to be sure to have the proper entertainment in your hospital bag. Like, all the electronics. Charge your iPads. Bring your cords. Because you're gonna need something to entertain you through the anxious, uncomfortable boredom you'll experience being induced for the first time.

At this point, the Pitocin was going, and the epidural was in, so the only thing left to do was break my water. They prepped me with towels under my butt, since this could be a huge mess otherwise. I was afraid this would hurt, ya know, since my doctor had to go right up in there to get the thing done. (By this point though, I think it's obvious I was scared for all of it.) But I didn't feel anything, except a warm rush all over the bed. They changed out the towels, put in a catheter, and I was left to sit and wait.

When you're in the hospital bed, you don't get to just kinda lay there and wait for the baby to make its way down your vagina. You'll be wearing a belt around your belly the whole time that allows the nurses to monitor your contractions and the baby's heartbeat. The speed and intensity of your contractions help them monitor the health of your baby and dose you with the proper amount of drugs to keep the induction going.

I was propped on one side, and the nurse helped me switch sides every hour or so. Maybe more often. And I'd be lying if I told you I remembered why I had to lay on my side. I would like to say it helps your cervix open, but I couldn't be completely sure that's the reason. The rough part about the epidural is that, pretty soon, you're not only numb but you also can't easily move your legs. It's gradual, but by the end of both births, I wasn't able to adjust the position of my legs at all.

So, let's go back to the 'Princess Package' that my doctor so lovingly provided for me while giving birth. Supposedly with the Princess Package, you aren't really going to feel contractions. Since you get your epidural so soon, contractions aren't starting until you already have the epidural in. But as labor progresses, your contractions get stronger, and sometimes you can feel them even through the epidural, depending on how high of a dose you have. You can have your epidural upped throughout the day, but only by so much, so often. Since I was propped up on one side, I'd feel contractions only on one side of my body. When you're lying down, the epidural tends to be heavier on the side you're lying down on. That's the reason for switching from one side to another, so the drugs will eventually even out again for a while. But you may feel contractions only on the side with less of the epidural flowing.

Brooklyn's labor lasted eight hours. I started feeling some contractions 5-6 hours in. Some of them brought me to tears, but most of them weren't that bad. It was just incredibly uncomfortable since I wasn't able to actually move my body with numb legs.

We haven't even addressed one of the worst parts of induction though.

You're not supposed to eat! Only ice chips and water. Certainly not suitable for a pregnant woman who wants to eat her anxiety in a bag of potato chips or a cheeseburger. I was definitely hungry, but more than anything I wanted something as a distraction. Kyle, of course, could eat. He offered to eat out in the lobby or restaurant since it didn't seem fair that I watch him eat when I couldn't. It didn't bother me though, because that hospital room would have been way too lonely.

With that thought, I want to give a huge mid-book shout out to any woman who is doing this by herself. It's incredibly brave, and you're amazing. The hospital stay can be fearsome, but you will do great!

Throughout the day, the nurse would come and check my progress. Not only did she monitor how close contractions were, but every couple of hours she'd check to see how much I was dilated and effaced. There were several times she had to just come and fix my contraction belt because it slipped off and wasn't tracking progress anymore. It seemed like I actually stopped progressing at some point, so they upped my Pitocin, and we were on track again. She also realized toward the end of the day, as Brooklyn's head started to protrude, that she was 'sunny side up' or in a posterior position, with her head facing away from my back. The ideal position for delivering a baby is the anterior position, with her head facing down towards my back.

To fix that, my doctor had to rotate her in the womb. I can't imagine how that would have felt if I didn't have an epidural. I also can't imagine what my husband was thinking when my doctor was elbow deep in my vagina turning our baby around.

After some sarcastic comments to my doctor and a little more time, they decided it was time to push around 4:30 pm.

You will also be able to tell when it's 'go time.' It literally feels like the baby is going to slide right out of your butt. And, I hate to tell you, but the rumors are true. You might poop in the hospital bed. I didn't with Brooklyn, but I did with Charlie. And not even when I was actually pushing. I was just lying there, and it came right on out. Your lower body is numb so you may not know right away...but you'll know. I felt gross and embarrassed to tell the nurse what was going on so she could help, but ya know what? It's real life. If the cost of receiving a human child is pooping in front of your husband, doctor and two nurses—so be it! (This is why it may be a good idea not to have any other family in the room.)

My memory of the actual pushing of the baby is noisy. It feels frantic. Though in reality, I don't think it was frantic in a scrambling kind of way. It may have been a build-up of emotion since I was feeling all the things at this point: anxious, excited, relieved, scared. But when it was go-time for me, there wasn't much waiting, since she was about ready to come out. My nurses called the doctor, and they got all the equipment ready to give her a thorough check-up.

They helped me sit up to get ready to push, which was a hefty task in itself considering my legs were completely immobile at this point, and the doctor directed the nurses to hold my legs up. Actually, he directed Kyle to hold one of my legs...I think he was too stunned to say no, probably feeling the same frantic rush of emotions and chaos as me. He did as he was told and got a VIP ticket to the birthing show that he never asked to attend.

To push a baby out, you have to push through the contractions. If you can't feel them, the nurse will let you know when one is happening. You hold your breath and push. The nurses I had did a great job of coaching me through when to start and stop.

Pushing out a baby was very intuitive for me, and I only pushed for five to ten minutes with both my girls. You can go to some classes that teach laboring and pushing techniques, which would probably be more helpful than anything you'd read in a book. A friend told me that during her labor, they brought in a mirror for her to observe what she was doing when she pushed. The visual connection between what you're trying to do can help for some women. I wouldn't worry about this part. Between your own intuition and coaching from your nurses and doctor, you'll be just fine!

While you're pushing, your doctor may ask if you want an episiotomy like he did with me. He made a small slice on my perineum so Brooklyn could pass through. According to my doctor, "it was the only thing holding her in there," so I went ahead and did it. Some doctors may have different views on this, but I would personally rather have a clean cut that can be sewn together than try to push and have it rip on its own. (This is something to talk to you doctor about ahead of time!)

Pushing went unexpectedly fast for me. And we were basically done after the episiotomy. I also didn't realize that once you push the baby out to like the shoulders, the doctor just maneuvers them out.

You may ask, how do I know this if I can't see what's happening down there? Because my doctor basically made Kyle take pictures. Yea, weird right? Well, my doctor is kind of a goofy guy, which is why I like him. He told Kyle, "You want a video? Come on! Get on in there!" Kyle may have been temporarily relieved of the task of holding my leg up, though I'm pretty sure he was just in autopilot at this point. So, he snapped some live pictures of Brooklyn coming out, the thought of which still mortifies me to this day. Seriously shuddering just thinking about them. We reviewed them once together, looked at each other with a grimace, and deleted them from his phone. And all traces of the iCloud. Forever. There is no reason for me to revisit those images, especially now that they're seared in my brain forever.

There were only two more 'traumatic' moments for us left.

Kyle, having really gotten the grand husband experience so far, got one more honor he didn't ask for. Cutting the umbilical cord. This was not something he ever imagined doing. He recalls it being 'very rubbery.' After that, I think he hid behind my hospital bed, so the only thing left to do was receive the baby. In hindsight of all this, you might want to write out anything your husband should or should not be doing in your birthing plan.

The second traumatic moment was for me, which was when my doctor, without asking, set Brooklyn down on my belly. Straight outta the womb. Covered in a slimy white coating and amniotic fluid. I swear, from the eyes of a shell-shocked mother in labor, the scariest looking humans are babies that have emerged from the placenta. Like a hallucination, you don't know what you're looking at, or who you're looking at, even though you've been with that person for the last nine months. It is the strangest thing I ever experienced. Fresh babies have reddish-purple skin, and their faces are swollen. They can be really wrinkly. Sometimes they have slightly misshapen heads, depending on how they exited the canal. And they are covered in that white coating, which is a protection layer from all the fluid in the womb. For me, it was like looking at a stranger. I'd bet it is not like that for many women. Some women feel more connected to their babies in the womb, but I was not that woman. And I'm telling you this because it is 100% okay to feel like your baby kinda freaks you out.

After actually giving birth, we spent about another hour or so in the delivery room. The nurses and on-call pediatrician spent some time getting Brooklyn's vitals, making sure there were no obvious birth defects or issues and cleaning her up. While Brooklyn was being tended to, so was I. My doctor made sure that the full placenta was removed, and then I had to get stitched from the episiotomy. I don't remember when my epidural got turned off, but I'm pretty sure it was before this point, though I couldn't feel getting stitches because enough of the meds were still in my system at that point.

Once Brooklyn was ready, they brought her over to me for skin-to-skin time and an immediate feeding. The first few days of breastfeeding are baffling for many reasons. For example, the fact that a baby is born knowing they're 'supposed' to suck on your boob is just weird. How humans (or any animal) is born with instincts like that is just incredible. Two, that your body just starts producing colostrum, and that the measly little drops of colostrum that come out are somehow 'enough' for your baby. Colostrum is the thicker, gold fluid that comes out before your milk fully comes in, and it is basically a baby superfood. You won't produce much, but it will be enough.

The whole situation is just surreal. There you are, with your boobs out in front of people, and another human sucking on them, with nurses and whoever else you let in the room standing around to watch you fumble through it. The nurses will often offer you help with this, especially if you're a first-time mother. They'll not only help properly position the baby, but also properly position your boob in the baby's mouth. Which means, they're grabbing your boobs. I am sure some are gentler than others, but some of them just stick the nipple right on in there.

That first feed doesn't last very long, and you're left with skin-to-skin time with your baby. I wish I had more touching words for you about this moment. Of course, I was happy and excited, but it was otherworldly. Obviously, all women will have a better or worse version of this experience to varying degrees. I wanted to enjoy it more than I did, and that was because I started feeling severe lower back pain. Turning a baby in the womb can be a painful experience, and since I had my epidural, I didn't feel a thing. But once it wore off, the pain I had from it was excruciating. I had to give Brooklyn back because I couldn't focus. It was after 5 pm, and I hadn't eaten all day long, so I couldn't take any pain medication either.

We had to wait a bit longer before we could go up to our room. I don't remember why, but it was likely some time to get us officially admitted. Eventually, they helped get me in a wheelchair so our new family of three could make our way up together.

I had to eat so I could get mediation for my back pain, so we immediately called in to room service. I ordered a chicken quesadilla. It took at least 30 minutes to get delivered. When it arrived, I got situated in my hospital bed and Kyle positioned the table over my lap.

Then he lifted the lid off the quesadilla, we looked at each other and burst out laughing. It was quite possibly the smallest quesadilla ever made, and of course, it came with no salsa or guacamole. I scarfed it down so I could pop my pills, and Kyle immediately found a pizza place that would deliver to the hospital.

I really should have known better than to trust hospital food. When we had our baby classes, the instructor made a joke about having people come visit you in the hospital. She said, "People always ask if they can bring you anything. And you should always say yes because there's a Chick-fil-A around the corner." She wasn't just trying to be funny, but also give some really great advice!

The hospital you choose might have a better room service scene, but just in case, you should be prepared with some snacks, and a wish list of food for your visitors to bring. Bringing you food is one of the best way friends and family can help out.

I don't remember whether it was before or after the quesadilla incident, but somewhere in there, I felt the urge to pee. Mind you, I hadn't felt this urge all day since I was numb from my lower back down and had a catheter. I had to call the nurse in to relieve my bladder for a couple of reasons. The first and more pressing was that I still couldn't walk that well with some of the numbness still hanging around. You might be thinking, surely Kyle could have helped me to the bathroom. He wasn't still in shock from his iPhone documentary of your first child's birth, was he?

No, he wasn't. You need a nurse because they have to monitor the volume of pee you can produce after giving birth. They essentially put a measuring cup made to fit in a toilet under the seat and make sure that you urinate a certain number of fluid ounces before you're cleared. This helps assure that everything down there is working properly again after the trauma it just experienced, along with the epidural.

Not only was my urethra possibly traumatized, but I was as well. I was scared to go pee. At first, my muscles didn't seem to want to work, and even though I felt like I had to go, and I was telling my body to go, it took me a few minutes to actually go. Mostly, I thought it would hurt because everything was swollen, raw and aching.

Sanitation is a different beast after birth. Wiping yourself up with toilet paper is not an option for quite some time. But don't worry, there are super awkward alternatives! The hospital provides you with squirt bottles to clean yourself up instead. So, before you pee, you're spending several minutes at the sink trying to get the water to the right temperature so that when you need to squirt yourself clean, you're not cringing. It is a treat. It is also necessary to make sure you don't feel gross and to have any potential stitches you had to have stay clean.

Now could also be a good time to address the diaper situation. That's right, ladies. Not only did you just give birth to a tiny human who needs to wear tiny diapers, but you yourself will be wearing diapers, too. Those diapers are not tiny. I got dressed in the biggest pad you've ever seen in your life. The size of a kitchen towel folded in half. I then put on this very soft, very stretchy boy short underwear to help hold it up.

After trying to go pee for the first time, wearing a diaper made sense. I'm not sure you need much detail around that, but you basically have nine months' worth of a period needing to exit your body. It might seem like you're bleeding a lot, and that's because you probably are. If it is ever concerning to you or looks weird, just talk to your nurse! They will help you understand all of the nitty-gritty details and make sure you're comfortable and healthy.

If you thought talking about your own diapers and urine volume was kinda gross, I hate to tell you that we're not done with the gross stuff. And if you thought we'd be done talking about poop after the whole delivery room cost-of-birthing-a-human situation, you are wrong.

I was scared to pee, but I was even more terrified of pooping. And through my embarrassment, I forced myself to talk to the nurse about it. I didn't poop until the next day after having Brooklyn, and I actually asked my nurse if it was okay to go. She laughed with me a little bit and said if I was scared of tearing out my stitches, I didn't need to worry because that wouldn't happen. Nonetheless, my downstairs business was aching and raw, and pooping and then cleaning myself up was way too much to think about.

Constipation can also be an issue. It was with Brooklyn, and even worse after having Charlotte. I actually didn't poop for like 3 or 4 days after Charlotte! As it turns out, the pain medication they were giving me caused constipation—a little side effect that I was not informed about. After being home with Charlotte for a full day, I called the nurse about my problem. And she scared the (figurative) shit out of me. She said if I didn't poop within the next 12 hours that I needed to go to the emergency room. I was already on edge with a newborn at home. Layering this potentially alarming situation on top of it didn't help. Naturally, I freaked out.

I sent Kyle to CVS to get ibuprofen (so I could stop taking the narcotics my doctor prescribed), stool softener, milk of magnesia and some more giant pads, because I had used up everything that I brought home from the hospital. My loving husband came home with all the good stuff and didn't even say how awkward he felt picking up such an embarrassing purchase.

I loaded myself up with everything the nurse had recommended on my call, and close to 8 hours later I still hadn't pooped. I called her back because I had a feeling an ER visit was a little extreme. She then elaborated, that sometimes after giving birth your organs can get shifted around and prevent you from digesting properly. An ER visit is only really required if you have pain, which I didn't have, I just felt backed up. Oh, and some hemorrhoids, which was fun to add to the mix. It would have been helpful for her to clarify that on the original call, so I'm providing it to you in case you run into this issue, too. Maybe a normal person would ask on the first call, do I still go if I'm not in pain? But a sleep-deprived newborn mom doesn't always think that far ahead. Hopefully these awkward paragraphs in my book can save you a call to a nurse talking about poop.

It's all gross. I know. I KNOW! And women don't want to acknowledge these things because of that. But it's real life, ladies. This is the shit we go through.

I think we've officially checked all the bodily fluids off the list of things to talk about, so…moving on! I'm probably almost done being gross. Let's go back to the rest of the hospital stay.

If you follow any pregnant influencers on Instagram, you might see them in a hospital bed, perfectly posed wearing a really cute outfit. My reality was quite different, and honestly, I was more comfortable wearing the hospital gown for roughly the first 24 hours I was admitted. In fact, I didn't shower until the next afternoon. I was told not to shower until after my IV port was taken out, which was done the next afternoon. The thought of showering also felt like a lot of work, considering the pain I was in. Even the next day, my back still hurt, and it was not comfortable to walk. When I finally did shower, Kyle had to help me get in and out, and help towel me off, because I couldn't bend down to reach my legs. Another beautifully humbling moment in our marriage.

I don't mean to scare you about the vaginal pain after having a baby. Realistically though, you can't expect a quick rebound, all things considered. But there is some management for the pain. For starters, you can have ibuprofen again after having a baby, so no more acetaminophen which doesn't really do much at all! (At least for me, it couldn't knock out a pregnancy headache worth a damn.) There are also soothing foams and witch hazel pads that will help ease your pain. You know what else my nurses brought me? Icicle diapers. Diapers that are filled with water and then frozen! Place 'em between your legs, underneath your own diaper. It helped me a lot in those first 24 post-partum hours.

For me, the recovery was infinitely more difficult than the birth itself. In hindsight, the birth was actually over pretty quickly. Recovery can last up to a couple of weeks, which—when you're sleep-deprived and taking care of a newborn—can feel like an eternity.

In general, Kyle and I were both ready to leave the hospital after the first day. Standard admission after vaginal birth is two nights, and three for a c-section. Even though it was great to have help from the nurses, it would also be great NOT to have help from the nurses. As a first-time mom, they'll pop their heads in every couple of hours to see if you need anything and to make sure that you're feeding your newborn often enough. Some of them will have you wake your baby up after 2-3 hours for a feeding. You should and will develop your own philosophy around this, depending on your comfortability, but both our babies were just fine on weight and we certainly did not want to wake a sleeping baby. Your baby might sleep a lot in the first 24 hours, which is typical of newborns. It was kind of a blessing actually. A sweet 24-hour grace period into motherhood. But that second day, be prepared for lots of feedings! And maybe little sleep.

The nurses at the hospital are helpful. They'll ensure you're breastfeeding properly, which many first-time moms need help with. (You can also see a lactation specialist with your pediatrician if you need extra help! I saw one the first time around, and even though it was helpful, I still decided to stop after a couple of weeks.) They will also help you with general care for your baby. They offer to do the first bath, change the diapers, and anything else you might need. But as you can imagine, the hospital bed is cumbersome, your husband is probably sleeping on a couch and the comforts of home might help put some new-parent anxiety at ease. Between check-ups from your doctor, tests on your baby, blood draws, filling our birth certificate paperwork, feedings and little sleep, the hospital stay, in general, can be a bit overwhelming.

You might also be more comfortable taking visitors once you get home. We only had a few visitors during our hospital stay. The rooms are not that big, and it can get crowded and loud pretty quickly. We had set up a two-hour window where we allowed visitors in (this was actually the reason I showered and changed) and asked most people to visit us once we got settled at home.

When you are ready to leave, I would advise asking the nurse to get check-out started early in the day. It can take a while! You have to wait for the pediatrician to do an assessment of your baby and you need clearance from your doctor. There's also a bunch of paperwork.

The last tip I have for the hospital stay is to load up on all the newborn diapers in your room. Stash them in your bag to take home. You will need them!

My story is unique to me but might help you get through your own experience. You might have a c-section, or have your baby come so fast that you don't have time for an epidural. (This happened to a dear friend of mine, and I'll tell you, I was terrified for it to happen to me.) You're going to have varying amounts of joy and happiness than I expressed, and there will be different things that might freak you out.

Regardless of how you give birth, the weirdest part about the hospital stay is the part where you leave. You'll be pushed in a wheelchair, put your newborn in the car seat, and start to drive home. With one more human than when you arrived. It's literally a moment like, "They're letting us take this kid? We're trusted with another human life? What the hell are we doing?"

There is no chapter of figuring out how to take care of your baby. You will jump right into the thick of it. The highlight of those first few weeks is a lot of emotion—and not the high-serotonin-level kind. Sure, there is a practical guide to taking care of your baby, but you're about to be deep in the trenches, fighting for normalcy, and taking small victories along the way.

7 BEING HOME WITH YOUR NEWBORN

Emily: How do you split baby duties with your husband?

Me: Like bottles and diaper changes?

Emily: Right now, I'm doing everything myself in the morning until I pass out at 10 pm. Then I ask Tim to take over and do the midnight feeding, 3 am and 6 am.

Me: When I was on maternity leave, I pretty much did everything except for bottles/diapers between 7 pm and 11 pm. Sometimes, my husband would take over until midnight.

Emily: Damn. That sounds hard.

Me: It is.

Emily: I just feel like we are both unhappy and tired all the time, so I was wondering if there was a better way to do things.

Me: It's kind of just the way it is with a newborn. Which really sucks. You need to figure out what works best for you, even if all the options are not great options.

The Reality of Maternity Leave

This was a real conversation with a friend, when she expressed feeling unhappy and tired all the time with her newborn. How drab is that? Unfortunately, that resonates with me. It's the hapless truth about raising a newborn.

Being home with a baby, whether you are working or on maternity leave, can be a complete and utter drain. I'll give you four reasons why.

Fatigue. You're gonna be tired. It's astonishing that I could even function on the number of hours I slept in the first month with Brooklyn. The lack of sleep takes a physical toll on your body. Someone will tell you 'sleep when she sleeps,' and you may want to spit in their face because it's nearly impossible to do. I have never been one to fall asleep easily except in my own bed at night. Naps are not a thing I can do. Kyle would constantly scold me for being tired, but in turn not napping enough. I don't think he believed that I actually tried and couldn't. But even if you are able to nap on command (so jealous of those with that superpower), it's inevitable that the moment you lay down...the baby will wake up. It's almost laughable how often that happens. I mean, you probably would laugh if you weren't so pissed off that it happened four times in a single day.

Hunger. You're gonna be hungry. Hunger can also take a toll on your body, and sometimes you'll forget to eat. I love food, and I never understood a person could be so busy they'd skip a meal—until I had a baby. There were definitely days when I'd look up at the clock, see it was 2 pm and realize I hadn't eaten a single thing that day! (That might be different if you're breastfeeding—I've heard that breastfeeding hunger can be more ravenous than the third trimester of pregnancy!) But it's so easy to be caught up in diaper changes, feeding, laundry and dishes that you don't actually know the last time you had a real meal. Let alone sat at a table with someone and enjoyed it.

Lethargy. You're also gonna be...lazy—for lack of a better word! Obviously, you're busy AF, so lazy isn't quite right. But it can be hard to find time to exercise, which you aren't even cleared to do for the first 4-6 weeks post-partum. If your baby is a fussball like Charlotte was, you're probably not getting much physical activity in after you are cleared, aside from non-stop holding and bouncing your baby. Exercise brings me life. It is my main form of stress relief which is part of what made pregnancy and maternity leave so hard. Neither phase of life allowed me to exercise as freely as I once had. Exercise might sound like it'd make you more exhausted, but that is definitely not the case for me!

Stress. Now we've got a snowball effect going on. One type of stress will build on another. Not having a proper form of stress relief can bring on physical pain, like headaches and backaches. And all that combined, with being home on baby duty, takes an emotional toll on you as well.

Caring for a baby on your own cannot only be stressful, but it can be lonely.

You might feel infinitely lonely. Your doctor might warn you about the 'baby blues.' I hate this terminology. It's a politically correct way of saying you'll be losing your shit on an emotional roller coaster as your hormones work their way out of your body, leaving you to dizzily navigate your way through a foreign amusement park called Motherhood, and no one provided a map.

I want to make a note here that I am not referring to post-partum depression. That is a different beast of its own that your doctor can help you with. If you need to know the difference, talk to your doctor.

Loneliness took me by surprise on my first maternity leave. I figured I'd be perfectly content simultaneously watching my baby sleep, and also the entire series of One Tree Hill. The ultimate dream, right? To be lazy on the couch with nothing to do? It might have been the dream when I was in college, but unfortunately, it no longer was. One Tree Hill turned into the entire series of Friends. And long walks by myself in our little neighborhood. And staring at a baby who couldn't talk back.

And then, wishing my maternity leave was over after the third week so I could go back to work and be near humans again

A lesson I learned after I lived it—it's important not to drown out your loneliness with a Netflix binge and watching the clock tick away until your husband gets home.

I did this every day on my first leave. I got myself pent up with anxiety, having nothing to do but care for one small child. I craved human interaction. And when Kyle got home, I had nothing other than a recap of diaper changes and tears to contribute to our conversation. He was tired. I was tired. And I had to go to bed early so I could get up for feedings. The interaction I had with him was essentially non-existent and I felt like a useless member of society.

After a while, I made it a point to actively do things that might prevent me from getting so lonely. It didn't always involve human interaction, but small things did make a big difference.

Here are some suggestions for you, as these are things that helped me:

- Try to put yourself together in the morning, even if it just means brushing your hair and putting on jeans with nowhere to go. Sitting in your pajamas or workout gear all day can make you feel worthless.
- Get outside. Even though long walks might feel a little lonely after a while, I do think that getting in a good dose of sunshine can make you feel better, or at the very least count as a small workout to make you feel productive.
- Find errands to run. Getting out of the house for one small errand every day can help pass the time and give you a bit of human interaction. Lay off Amazon Prime and load up on trips to Target!
- Find someone to talk to. Facetime another friend who you know might be home. Text your friends about how you're feeling. Find a new mom's group in the neighborhood. Visit your husband or partner at work and go to lunch.

This last recommendation is the most important. When you're lonely, you need someone to talk to.

I learned that while it is always a good idea to talk to your husband about how you're feeling (because—hello!—communication is one of the pillars of a good marriage), it may not be a good idea to text your husband every time the baby is inconsolable, has a blowout, refuses a bottle, won't nap…the list goes on. It will not only make him stressed out for you but stressed because he can't help. You probably live in the United States, so he is back at work almost immediately since paternity leave (let alone a decent maternity leave) isn't a thing that usually exists.

I'm not just speculating he'll feel this way. I know because my own husband told me. I did this with Charlotte. In our two months of colicky disillusion, I was constantly texting Kyle. All-day long. He's my person and he is supposedly half responsible for our children. We talk about everything. Naturally, I'd go to him when I just needed to tell someone that the baby was driving me crazy.

But he finally told me how much stress that was putting on him. That stress was resulting in him not being productive at work, let alone the constant distraction I was creating for him. That stress then was causing him to lose sleep, which wasn't fair to either of us or our toddler because she needed at least one parent who wasn't on the brink of an internal meltdown.

Believe me, he's thinking about you and baby all the time. If he doesn't hear from you all day, I guarantee he will check-in. No need to alert him about the baby's fifth poop of the day.

I'm not saying you can't complain to your husband. It's gonna happen. But reaching out to someone else who will sympathize with you, like your own mother, sister, best friend—whoever, even if they don't have kids—may be more helpful because they are also part of your support system. They are there for you. And they are not the ones who will be walking into a newborn warzone after they finish work for the day.

Maternity leave is certainly no vacation. And the reality is that there is no equal split between parents when one person is on leave and the other one isn't.

For Emily, unhappy and tired came from the splitting of childcare duties itself. For me, the unhappy feelings were the loss of connection with my husband for a time.

And tired? It's an inevitable thing regardless of the situation.

Whether you are lucky enough to get a paid maternity leave or not, it's a full-time job with unpaid overtime.

At least, I treated it as my new full-time job. I got 8 weeks paid leave with Brooklyn and 6 weeks paid with Charlotte, and each time I approached it as my job. Kyle took one week of vacation each time which was infinitely helpful, but after that, I was mainly on my own. Timing with Charlotte was not great. She was born when he was busier than ever with work. He had no one to cover for him, so after a week of vacation, he was scrambling to get caught up.

After his week of vacation with Charlotte, I felt like I never saw him anymore. There were some nights that Kyle would work late and not be home until 7 pm to relieve me of childcare duties, since I had both kids after Brooklyn was done with school.

Sure, THAT was hard. In a sleep-deprived state, taking care of a newborn and a toddler is a true test of motherhood, even if it is only for a couple of hours a night. But that phase didn't last long, and it was necessary. Necessary because Kyle was working a job that helped pay our bills. He was working long hours at his day job, and I was working long hours at my mom job.

What was even harder than the non-stop caring of a newborn and some single-mom duty, though, was barely seeing my husband for weeks, even if he wasn't late. It was a time clock we developed to give me some relief from mothering. The difference with Kyle working full-time, and me working full-time mothering, is that mothering a newborn means day shift and night shift. Kyle took a small swing shift.

He'd get home between 6 and 7 pm.

I'd go to bed between 7:30 pm and 8:00 pm.
He took care of baby until 10-11 pm.
I'd be on duty and then ideally, he'd sleep until leaving for work at 7 am.

Kyle always told me to ask for help so I wouldn't drown, and this was the best method we could come up with. I did some pumping, but we did a lot of formula. I hated breastfeeding and I hated pumping even more. This was a decision I made so I could get some relief in the evening. It was 'easy' enough for Kyle to do a bottle and put Charlotte to sleep. But the downside was that I wouldn't see Kyle for more than one hour a day.

This seclusion from my husband is what stands out to me the most from each of my maternity leaves. Even on my toughest days of no naps, crying baby and diapers, I'd cry too, not just because mothering was hard, but because I missed my normal relationship with Kyle.

Everyone splits baby duties differently according to what works best for their family. There is no single right way to do it. The important part is that YOU are okay with the way you have chosen to split duties. Or not split duties. I didn't believe it was fair to ask Kyle to do anything during the middle of the night because he did have to get up for work the next day. Even though that meant life would be harder for me. And that meant sacrificing any time we'd have to spend together during the week. Neither of us was living a great quality of life between baby and work.

Did I want him to do a 1 am bottle? Hell yea, I did! But he still had a job to go to, and then come home and help out with a baby for four hours, which isn't easy either. It's really hard to put yourself in your partner's shoes when you're exhausted and tripping around on the baby seats and blankets and burp rags that are laying around your house.

Children are a test on a marriage. Marriage requires so much more work after kids are involved.

We may have both been unhappy at times, but at least only one of us was really, truly tired.

But there will be a light at the end of the tunnel. It will end. You will not have a newborn forever, and you will not have a weird, crazy sleep schedule that you can't handle forever.

You'll need to remember and remind yourself that this time is very temporary. People tell you that, but when you're living it, it's easy to forget. I had to remind myself each day that I barely got to interact with another adult. It will end, and you just have to take it one day at a time.

You'll be unhappy and tired.

But you'll realize it isn't all the time. And it is only *for* a time.

It's also important to remember to ask for help when you need it. And do you know when the best time to ask for help is going to be?

The weekend!

Even reading those words perk me up.

Yes, moms may need to pick up the brunt of the work that it takes to keep a house together during the week. But weekends are a time to get caught up because there is someone there all day long to help. All-day!

But ladies, the weekend will not work for you unless you make it work. You can't always assume someone knows what you want or need. Slamming cabinet doors as you empty the dishwasher or huffing and puffing up the stairs because you're changing a diaper (yet again!) is passive-aggressive and it is not the answer. That kind of behavior is only going to make everyone mad. You'll get frustrated. And your attitude is not going to come across well to others. I know from experience. Slamming a cabinet door screams 'leave me alone' more than it says, 'please help me.'

<u>Ask for Help</u>

Kyle would constantly tell me to ask for help if I needed it. For a long time, I didn't ask, because I just assumed, he would volunteer. But not all men—or people in general—are like that. In fact, they may think that since you're used to taking care of the baby during the day, you might just keep on doing it. Because you want to? Because the baby wants you to? I am not sure because I don't understand any of the logic of not volunteering.

Remember that whole 'communication is a pillar of a good marriage' thing? We often forget this in times of distress. Everyone is on edge and tired and life is different, and your feelings come out in the wrong way. It's how fights happen. So instead of assuming you'll automatically get the help you want, just ask for the help when you want it.

I had to realize there was a reason Kyle kept telling me to ask for help. It was because he would not notice I didn't want to everything by myself. I had to literally tell him, even if I thought it was glaringly obvious. So, if you find yourself in this situation...

Ask for help with the laundry that might have piled up during the week.

Ask for help with the dishes that have been sitting in the sink.

Ask your husband to feed and watch baby for an afternoon so you can take a three-hour nap, or workout, or actually leave the house to catch up with a friend. Yes! You can do this. You should do this. As early as you want and feel comfortable, because you need a break, too.

Better yet, get a babysitter and have a date night! We had our very first babysitters—Kyle's parents—when Brooklyn was two weeks old. It was our two-year wedding anniversary and my first time out of the house since giving birth to our precious newborn. We ate sushi and drank wine for three hours. Never mind that my boobs were ready to explode when I got home because I was still breastfeeding at the time. It was worth it because being able to spend quality time with my husband was just what I needed.

Leaving your baby with anyone that early may startle you. And it might feel like your heart is physically being ripped from your chest as you walk out the front door and leave your baby at home for the very first time. But I think the earlier you leave them, even just for a little while, the easier it is. It also helps you realize that the world is not all lost, and your life will find a new normal soon. It can help you regain a balance in your life. You need to remember to do a few things for yourself. Even though you have a baby to take care of, it is not your life's sole purpose to take care of the baby. You need to care for yourself, too.

Asking for help is not intuitive for everyone. But if you're drowning, you need a life raft. And once it's there, you need to trust in the person that's saving you. This might be your husband, your in-laws, your own parents, or anyone who wants to come see you.

Don't refold all the towels if they aren't tri-folded in the only way that makes them fit perfectly in your bathroom cabinets.

Don't worry if dishes haven't been properly pre-cleaned before entering the dishwasher, or if they were put away in the wrong places.

Don't hover over the person feeding your baby a bottle because you know that the optimal bottle position is at a 60% angle. Instead, remember that you are lucky to have someone who wants to help you. Be grateful for that and enjoy the time you get to rest.

There is only one time when you do worry—when you hover and properly train your life-raft-person to do things the right way.

That time is bedtime.

You will probably have tried several things to get your baby to sleep well at night. Some babies will sleep well regardless of the circumstance. But some babies must be swaddled in just the right way or have eaten just the right-sized bottle to go to sleep. If you have a baby who is particular about his sleeping situation, or even if your baby is sleeping through the night and it took you a long time to get there, then bedtime routine is the only time you lay down the law. You need to provide this person with instructions that are printed and mounted on the wall in your baby's room so that they are always easily accessible. (Not really, but really.) We've been through this a few times with an improper swaddling technique. I really should have mounted sample pictures on the wall.

Getting a baby to sleep at night is a huge triumph, and you don't want to come home from a date night, girls' night, or whatever it is that required a babysitter for your baby at night, and then have them wake up way too early.

<u>Expect the Unexpected</u>

So. Have I done a good job of making maternity leave sound completely miserable? It may seem obvious to some, but I think it is important to know your time off on maternity leave is not going to be easy. But there will be good times along with the bad, and you'll find your way through it!

I had two very different maternity leaves. They were both enjoyable and awful in their own ways.

Brooklyn was by all accounts an easy baby. This is what every single person told us from the beginning. I rolled my eyes at them, because even a good baby is hard sometimes, and I had zero other life experience with a baby. I did not grow up around babies, I didn't do much babysitting when I was in high school, and I had no older siblings with babies. I had nothing to compare her behavior to. To my benefit, Kyle did, and I leaned on him a lot in the first few weeks to figure out what the hell I was doing. I assumed I did everything wrong because she still cried sometimes.

The thing I didn't know is how much babies can cry, even over very small things. Remember, it their only form of communication! A lack of confidence and loneliness got the best of me the first month I was home. The house we lived in at the time at no natural light, and I'd sit in our living room, which was basically a cave, and stare at the clock until it was 5 pm. At 5 pm, I knew Kyle would soon be on his way home and things would be better. Kyle and I had only been married for two years at that point, and while we did have a great marriage, we were still really figuring out the best ways to talk to each other. Me, being a hormonal, emotional mess was really hard for both of us, let alone having another tiny, needy human in our house. I hated night feedings. I wished every day for time to pass more quickly so she would start sleeping longer. I wanted to be done with leave so I could go back to work.

But after that first month, our quality of life dramatically improved. Brooklyn put herself on a routine, and I was able to do things other than provide childcare. I started working on my blog several hours a day. I was able to work out and go for walks or go to Target to waste some time and wander around. And then she started to get interactive—smiling, grabbing at toys, cooing—and it was the best thing in the entire world. After 9 weeks, I did not want to go back to work. At all. We even, for a brief period, considered what it would take for me to not go back. (Spoiler alert, that didn't happen, though it was cute we thought we could make it work.)

I went into Charlotte's maternity leave so much more lighthearted. I knew what to expect out of raising a baby, and I knew that it would only be temporary. Getting up in the middle of the night was not as bad, and I was able to actually relax during the day because I was in a better mental space. It was kind of awesome.

At least, it was awesome at first. It went well for about two weeks, and I expected the rest of my leave to be the same. What I did not expect, was that she would start crying more each day. And then she was crying all day long. At her one-month check-up, we were told that a change to gentle formula might help. Out doctor said he hoped it wouldn't turn into full-fledged colic.

What. The hell.

How was it possible for a baby to just cry without end? No one knows. And that's why 'colic' exists. Colic is the inexplicable, inconsolable crying of a baby that can last up to six months. I was in complete disbelief that she'd just KEEP crying. It had to end at some point. I talked to a friend, who experienced something similar with her second baby. She let me know that colic isn't really a condition that you necessarily have to live with. You don't need to accept that there is no answer. There is likely always a reason your baby is crying, and with her advice, I refused to believe that she was just crying to torture me. She was crying because something was not right, and we had to fix it.

We spent the next month of her life trying to find a solution to our colicky problem. We tried gas drops, probiotics, and different bottles. We tried burping her more. We bought an expensive cushion imported from the UK that let her sleep on her belly (with close supervision, of course, please no one freak out). We tried silicone whistles that we greased up with Vaseline and stuck in her butt to help her pass gas and poop more often. (Yes, this is a real product. You can find it at Target.) We tried a total of five different formulas.

During that time, we also noticed that Charlotte's poop was changing. (You should just get comfortable talking about poop from this day forward. You'll be doing it a lot.) It was no longer looking like normal baby poop. It was very thick and very dark. Almost black. I knew this wasn't right, so I called the pediatrician and spoke to their nurses about it. Twice. We were informed to try a different formula, but then wait it out.

It's unclear whether the nurse actually talked to Charlotte's doctor and described everything that was going on. When Kyle took Brooklyn into our pediatrician for her 2.5-year check-up about three weeks after I called the office, Kyle talked to him directly about Charlotte's problems. Our doctor told us we should save a sample to get tested because there is a chance there might be blood in it. If there was, that meant she was having trouble digesting cow's milk formulas, and we'd need to make another formula switch.

Do you know what? We tested her poop and there was blood in it. We switched to an elemental formula and within a few days, Charlotte was feeling better, crying less, and actually smiling.

It was truly heartbreaking for me to know she was crying because her little digestive system couldn't handle the food that we had given her. The elemental formula, which has all the milk proteins completely broken down, allowed her body to properly digest it. She was in pain the entire time, and although I understand diagnosing things like this in a newborn has to be a process because their tiny little bodies are so new and figuring themselves out, it pissed me off that we all had to go through two months of misery like we did.

We were also told by our doctor that most babies who have this problem will grow out of it and not develop an actual dairy allergy. When she was 10 months, we tested this out by feeding her some yogurt, making sure to have our Benadryl handy. Luckily, she had no actual dairy allergy, and her digestive system had matured enough by that point to handle the dairy proteins.

The main takeaway? It's okay if you frequently call or visit your pediatrician if you think something is wrong. And, if you experience digestive issues like this with your baby, know that it is not always permanent!

<u>Mom Guilt</u>

The bond between mom and baby can be calming for the baby, and sometimes, for you as a mother. But many times, it doesn't feel calming. Instead, it is demanding. My babies would cry as soon as I left a room. A few minutes would pass, and they'd have an 'out of sight, out of mind' experience. But as soon as I came back into their eyesight, it was bloody murder until I picked them up. My girls demanded for my attention all the time.

I, of course, was not on that level, easily holding back tears when I leave them, having become a fan of babysitters for my children early on. I'd be stressed out and eager to head out the door for date night, and later on in their life, send them to daycare. But as soon as I leave them, even now, I feel an emotional tug at my heartstrings. Often quite literally as soon as I close the door.

Even if maternity leave is as hard for you as it was for me, I encourage you to enjoy it as much as you can. It is filled with overwhelming emotion and frustration, but you will have plenty of the good feels, too. Soak it up. Because when you do go back to work, you'll experience a completely new set of emotions.

Enter: Mom guilt.

You might experience mom guilt in many different ways throughout your mothering career. There is a new mentality of addressing 'mom guilt' in a very progressive way—that is not giving in to it. And I agree! We moms have to do what we need to do to carry on our lives. We will make the decisions we have to make in the best interest of our children.

Sometimes, those decisions are small. It could mean feeding your children macaroni and cheese three or four times a week because it is in their best interest that you maintain your own sanity by feeding them the only food they willingly eat. There is no mental capacity for a battle over dinner every night. There should be no mom guilt in that!

But I think we have to at least acknowledge that many women feel mom guilt. And this will likely become most evident for you if you choose to enroll your children in daycare or hire help of any kind.

Note that I did not say, 'go back to work and enroll your children in daycare.' Whatever it is you're doing, or would rather be doing, that requires someone else to watch your kids, is no business of mine. I'm a firm believer that everyone needs a break from their children at one point or another, in whatever way they choose to do it.

I chose to go back to my full-time job. It was a financial decision for our family, and a fulfilling decision for me. I wanted to work. But even with compelling reasons to go back, the mom guilt was there.

My kids did, and still do, spend at least 9-10 hours at daycare every single weekday. That is what's required for me to accomplish everything I need to do in a day—to maintain my own health and well-being and excel in my career.

Daycare is the ultimate confliction of feelings. Emotional extremes. Highs and lows. Your heart will break knowing you get such little time with them during the day. But you might also feel the greatest relief dropping them off after a morning full of your child's screams and tears for not wanting to get dressed.

Bottom line, it sucks that you have so much less time with them when you go back to work. But not all our family circumstances are the same, and this is a choice some of us need or want to make. No choice is better than the other; it is simply what works best for your family.

<u>Finding Sanity</u>

After your maternity leave is over, whether you go back to work, or you begin to ease into stay-at-home motherhood, you need to figure out what routines are going to be best for you. You need to have some serious discussions about how life is going to go now that you're a family with children. What does that mean? It means, you need to set expectations with yourself and your partner and try to create a routine that works for the whole family.

Do not forget that (most of) you have a partner in all this.

It is tough to balance kids, work, a marriage and whatever else it takes to keep yourself together. One of these priorities is often bound to suffer if you don't ask for help and find a balanced routine that works for you. 'Setting expectations' might sound harsh, but it is something to consider doing with your partner. You want to set expectations for your roles in the family, and not be setting *assumptions*, like:

- Mom does all the chores around the house, or
- Mom does bedtime every night, or
- Mom picks up and drops off at daycare, or
- Mom does workouts after the kids are in bed instead of a more optimal time in the morning, or
- Mom always does the dishes, or
- Mom does all the sick days with the kids

Or, whatever else it is that keeps you busier than you want to be

I made this mistake, too. Both in setting reasonable expectations with myself, and with my husband.

Example One: The Overachieving Mom

Brooklyn was a relatively easy transition back to work. After 8 weeks of paid leave and one week of vacation, she was sleeping through the night. We made the decision that we'd alternate mornings of going to the gym and getting Brooklyn ready. We both had long commutes to work, so we were up early. Brooklyn was at daycare early, but it was working pretty well. Then eventually she started sleeping longer and longer, and an easier routine just fell into place. No longer unhappy or tired at all.

Going back to work with Charlotte was a shit show. I had made the decision to keep her home with me for a while. After 6 weeks of paid leave and one week of vacation, I was back at work two weeks earlier than I was with Brooklyn. Charlotte wasn't vaccinated yet, so we didn't want her in daycare. And since I have a job where I can work remotely, that meant working with Charlotte at home. My original decision was to work at home with her until she was 3 months old.

It was not one of my smarter decisions.

I don't know how many times Kyle told me we can just pay for daycare, considering we were still in the presence of a colic-monster child. She was also not yet sleeping through the night. But keeping her home seemed feasible. Maternity leave ended mid/late-October. We had family visiting for a week in November for Thanksgiving. I was also able to use some vacation time, but I just couldn't justify paying for daycare knowing I was at home.

This is one of the times in my life when I will admit that Kyle was right and putting her in daycare from the start would have been a smarter decision. Enrolling her in daycare would have been incredibly less stressful for me. I am stubborn and was bound and determined to save money by not enrolling her in daycare, which was really my main driver at that point, seeing as how hard it was to take care of her.

Example Two: The Mom Who Wanted Help but Didn't Ask

As I started at work again with my second child, I became what many people referred to as 'Supermom.' Working full time, caring for a baby full time, working out again, and cooking dinner on the reg. I was also caring for both kids on my own a couple of nights a week because Kyle's job often required after-hours events. From the outside, it seemed like I was rocking this whole mom-of-two thing, and there was no reason to ask for Kyle to be home for more regular hours.

But then came the day where I completely lost my shit.

Don't get me wrong, I had many breakdowns during maternity leave and starting work again. Charlotte still required one or two feedings at night, and I was tired. Mostly I would just cry, sometimes I yelled at Kyle. Sometimes, and I really hate to admit it, but I'd yell at Brooklyn. I knew I shouldn't, because she was just a toddler, but I was sleep-deprived and frustrated.

But there was a day when I was working and Charlotte would not shut the eff up, and I straight up screamed in her face for a good 15 seconds. Part of me couldn't believe I had done it, but part of me felt so much better afterward and wanted to do it over and over again. Because a screaming match with your baby is always the answer to our troubles.

I knew I was needing help and I wasn't getting it. And that is because I wasn't asking for it. I hadn't asked Kyle to start helping with night feedings after I went back to work. Maybe I thought I had asked, but I really wasn't asking loud enough, because I was still the only one getting up with Charlotte in the middle of the night.

The day after my screaming match with Charlotte, she woke up crying (as babies do) at 3 am and 6 am. After feeding her, I came back into our room and just sobbed. I told Kyle, "I know God only gives you as much as you can handle. But I just don't think I can take this anymore."

That was a turning point for us, and Kyle realized his priorities had to shift back to family from work. I finally told him I needed it to happen, which I should have done much earlier, instead of trying to just do everything all by myself. I had assumed that he'd work less and volunteer to get up at night, but it didn't happen. I was working from home, and it was assumed I was handling it just fine. Once it became clear I was a wreck, he was more than willing to take on more baby duty.

After that, a routine that we could both manage finally worked itself out. Charlotte became less colicky once we realized her dairy-based formulas were tearing up her insides. We started her on the 'elemental' formula that cost eight times as much money but cost us all far less emotional grief as her constant crying subsided.

Charlotte started daycare at three months old. She was not yet sleeping through the night, but life was much more manageable. (This sleeping pattern, by the way, is TOTALLY normal. Brooklyn, from what I understand, was a fluke baby sleeping through the night so early. It only set me up for awful expectations the second time around.) Charlotte was happier, which make us happier. We were also alternating night shift with baby, which was a great balance that we both agreed worked.

Being home with a newborn takes a lot of patience, and so does everything else that happens after your maternity leave! No two experiences are the same—even your own experiences from one maternity leave to the next. Below are a few questions answered by women about being home with a baby. These are real highs and lows that women experienced and provide a realistic picture of how construed maternity leave can be compared to someone who hasn't gone through it. Some of this you will likely relate to on your own leave!

What was your favorite part about maternity leave?

- Getting newborn snuggles
- Not having to work!
- Getting quality time with my baby and time to heal physically

after giving birth
- Having time to nurture my child and transform physically and mentally into motherhood
- Being paid to stay home
- Learning everything about being a new mom
- Not feeling like you have to get dressed every day
- Just being at home
- Having time to bond with my baby, and let my body recover. I didn't feel like myself again for a long time.

What was the hardest part about maternity leave?

- Feeling like I wasn't 'contributing' to anything other than being a mom
- Paternity leave isn't as generous, so I was alone for most of it
- Boredom and feeling unproductive at everything besides taking care of a baby
- Not getting enough pay
- The fatigue! And boredom.
- Lack of sleep, lack of personal time, and unpaid leave
- It's never long enough. I had 9 weeks the first time, and I will only get 6 weeks for my second leave.
- Feeling lonely
- Being alone, and the newborn crying. It was heartbreaking to listen to it and not know why it was happening.

What was your biggest struggle in the transition from maternity leave and going back to work or becoming a stay at home mom?

- Mainly finding a new routine! I was more than ready to go back to work.
- Keeping up with all things baby and house, and then adding in a job
- Handing my 2-month-old baby that I still didn't have figured out over to a stranger
- All the pumping!
- The fatigue, and cost of childcare

- Going from a full-time job of childcare to another full-time job of my paid job. From day to night, nonstop.
- On being a stay-at-home-mom, there is no consistent adult interaction anymore. There is no real reason to wear your nice clothes either.
- Finding the new balance and routine

8 SLEEP

Yep. I'm gonna do it. We're going to dedicate an entire chapter just to sleep. Because it's probably the number one thing that can solve all your problems, but also the thing that you can never get enough of in the first few months of your baby's life. Or for some, the first year. Or the first couple of years. My aunt once told me that they couldn't get my cousin to sleep through the night for three years. THREE whole years. That sounds like a hell only the devil himself could create.

My sleep schedule has been through different ups and downs my entire life. Although I've always been an early riser, I was definitely not always early to bed. As a kid, I'd say I got around 8 hours of sleep. In college? Four nights a week I was probably lucky to get five. Not because I was studying so much. Unless shot taking and binge-eating Taco Bell can get you through to graduation. (Maybe I am proof of that. Remember that whole 'get your life together' chapter? I needed that.) I actually prided myself on how much I could get done on such little sleep. I mean, I was a chemistry major, so there was actually a lot of studying, homework, test-taking and laboratory research to get done. Sleep was not a priority.

I honestly don't remember how much I slept during grad school, but somewhere between college and getting pregnant, I required at least a very specific 7.5 hours of quality sleep in order to feel human. Anything less would put me in a catatonic state by 3 pm. I can't claim that I would always wake up immediately refreshed, but after 10 minutes or so I'd be able to shake it off and feel good about my day. This feeling is something I soon realized wouldn't happen again for a while after I got pregnant, and subsequently had my baby. I mean, you KNOW it because that's the one thing everyone tells you.

Enjoy sleep now while it lasts!
Oh, you better get well rested before that baby comes!
Just wait until you're up all hours of the night!

Queue eye roll.

It's funny how people say these things to you so light-heartedly, like it's some big joke. Imagine if people said this to you when you had an actual newborn and weren't just pregnant. It would be a real reason to punch someone in the face. I might say that sarcastically, but I mean it sincerely. You don't realize how serious the sleep joke is until you experience it yourself.

Because sleep, as a mom, *is* a joke.

Do you know what the funniest thing about the sleep joke is? The fact that many of those people spouting these one-liners to you might be men. Men, who don't lose sleep at all during the actual pregnancy. They get the nine months leading up to the newborn-joke-sleep undisturbed. But you will lose sleep in those nine months. Maybe not the whole time, or maybe you will. The unpredictability of sleep from this point in your life forward is all part of the joke.

I pray that you don't have nausea so bad it keeps you up at night. Or leg cramps or sciatic pain. And that you'll be free from insomnia. I pray that your bed is more like a cloud than a mattress so that it can magically cuddle your belly in any position you choose to lay.

I pray you are not a back or belly sleeper. It's pretty obvious that you aren't supposed to sleep on your belly, but did you know you aren't supposed to sleep on your back either? The weight of the growing fetus and uterus can weigh down on your umbilical cord and slow blood flow to your baby. You'll notice you might get light-headed if you lay on your back for long enough. So, back sleeping! Gone.

I'm not sure why insomnia is a pregnancy symptom, but unfortunately, it is. Lying awake in the middle of the night next to your peacefully sleeping husband is not awesome but also very common. From months five through nine of both my pregnancies, I spent 3-4 nights a week lying in bed between 1 am and 4 am. Just lying there, staring in the darkness. Or Instagramming. I know you aren't supposed to stare into the depths of your iPhone for extended periods of time in the dark, but one woman can only take so much straight-up sleepless boredom. Also, my Kindle sat dead on my nightstand for two months because my pregnancy brain could never remember to charge it, so reading a book was not an option. There were certainly times when I'd just get up at 4 am and start my day with an episode of Grey's Anatomy DVRed from the week before. It was TV or Instagram because I was obviously not going to do anything productive that early in the day.

There were some days I would fall back asleep. Although, you know how sometimes when you wake up—wide awake—in the middle of the night, and then you actually do fall back asleep, only to wake up way worse off than you were before? That was basically my entire third trimester each time. It's shitty. The shittier part is you have a pregnancy-imposed caffeine restriction of 200 mg a day, so your next logical resort to keep yourself awake all day is having toothpicks hold your eyes open. The only thing you can do to help the situation is to have your freaking baby already.

See? Pregnancy sleep is a cruel joke.

Naivety had the best of me the closer we approached parenthood. I mean, I guess knew that babies would need to eat in the middle of the night. They made sure to tell us that in our hospital-required childcare class. (Even though, the fact that meant I'd have to wake up to a crying baby, didn't really click.) In your classes, they tell you, "Babies eat every 2 to 3 hours. And if they don't wake up after 3 hours, you should wake them up to eat to keep them nourished."

Um, what?

FALSE. (At least in my experience.) Please think twice before you ever wake a newborn baby. If you get your newborn to sleep for a four hour stretch in the middle of the night, you should be praising the heavens—because that means you got to sleep for at least three, if not more, of those four hours. Disclaimer statement before anyone raises hell: Of course, I do know there are those special cases when babies are born underweight or they are slightly malnourished because they have a difficult time feeding. This is why I ask you to 'think twice.' Your doctor or pediatrician may recommend this regardless of your baby's weight or health circumstance. Use your best judgment. Trust your gut!

We did not wake up our babies at night. They woke up plenty on their own, and your baby will, too. Let's remember this book is a satire and I am a doctor in Chemistry, not medicine, so anything I say cannot be taken for medical advice...but trusting your gut can go a long way as a parent.

All that to say, it's lucky as hell if you get more than a few hours of sleep in one stretch right off the bat.

So, how do you get a baby to sleep through the night?

Between patience and a good routine, you could accidentally turn off your baby monitor in the middle of the night, and as a result, unknowingly leave them to cry it out for two hours while you are sound asleep. Although you may simultaneously almost give yourself a heart attack.

Oh yes—this is another first-hand experience we stumbled upon. Though strangely, it worked in our favor.

When Brooklyn was 7 weeks old, she was going to bed at 10 pm and waking up around 3 am. (Please note we were told sleeping this long was highly unusual for such a young baby. #blessed.) One night, she woke up at 3 am per her usual schedule. I was exhausted (as many new mothers are) and watched the monitor for a couple of minutes to see if she would settle herself down or if I needed to queue up a bottle. She calmed herself down—or, so I thought—so I rolled over and went back to sleep. Well, little did I know that in my sleep-deprived state, I had actually turned the volume down all the way, which is why I didn't hear her cry through the monitor and thought she had stopped.

I woke up on my own at 4:30 am—truly amazed that my baby had slept so long! I had forgotten what it was like to wake up on my own, without a crying alarm clock. But then—I looked on the monitor. It had a color-coded soundbar, which was green when her room was quiet and ranged up to red when the sound was off the charts. This feature was designed to get a gauge on the sound coming from the room, without actually having to listen to it. What a silly feature for a zombie mom, right? When I woke up, the monitor's sound lights were quickly flaring all the way up from green to red—but I couldn't hear anything from the monitor. Realizing my mistake, I leaped out of bed and ran down the hall. I was appalled with myself, having let my baby cry for what could have been an hour and a half.

But then, the damnedest thing happened. As soon as I picked that baby up out of her crib, and laid her down on the changing table, her cries flipped off like a switch and she smiled at me.

Almost immediately.

It was in that moment that I realized the power struggle between mother and child. They cry, you jump. Even young infants can have magical, manipulative powers over you.

From that moment on, I never felt bad about letting my baby cry it out ever again.

You might be thinking, "But your baby was only 7 weeks old? Wouldn't she have been sleeping in your room, so that you could hear her?"

No. Nope. Absolutely not.

We were adamantly against having either of our babies sleep in our room for any period of time. Both of our babies slept in their crib from the first day they came home. We also knew that sleeping in the crib was safe, and we had little reason to worry something could happen, just because we were in a different room. This decision was made both for our own ability to fall asleep without a peeping baby, and to eliminate any difficult transition to a crib when she got older and more aware of her surroundings.

We have certainly become fans of the 'cry it out' technique. It can be hard, and parents will all do it in their own way. There are specific methods you can follow from professionals and self-proclaimed experts on baby sleep. In the end, you'll do what is best for you. You'll know what you can handle, and you'll learn what your baby can handle.

Our general rule of thumb was if our babies were full and had a clean diaper, but still wouldn't sleep, then we'd just let them cry. Of course, if they were sick, that's a different story. They definitely got extra cuddles and rocking then! But under normal circumstances, after no longer than thirty minutes, they would put themselves back to sleep. It wasn't always for as long as we'd want, but it at least got them used to calming themselves down.

There were a few times when we just had to turn the monitor off at night! Knowing that your baby is fine, but just won't sleep, can stress you out. They are not hungry. They do not have a dirty diaper. They aren't sick. But it is 1 am—and they are not sleeping…for us, the monitor went off. Occasionally, we would set an alarm to wake back up in an hour or so to check and make sure the crying fit was over. But more often than not, I would drift back in and out of sleep and turn the monitor back on after some time. This always worked for us, and we got more sleep because of it.

The truth is that getting a baby to sleep through the night can be a lot of trial and error. It turns out that babies are really particular, and even changing their bedtimes as little as 30 minutes can make a big difference. Although we were luckily blessed with a good sleeper with Brooklyn, Charlotte wasn't as easy. We were keeping her up later, in the hope that she'd sleep in that much longer. But strangely, we found that moving her bedtime from 8:30 pm to 7:00 pm got her sleeping longer! It's counterintuitive, but it worked.

Babies, as we know, are not like regular humans (a.k.a. people who like to get decent sleep). Keeping a baby up later does not necessarily mean they will sleep longer. We have found that keeping our children up later means they wake up earlier. And waking up earlier means waking up crankier. Trying this is certainly not in your best interest—especially once that baby becomes a toddler!

After trial and error, we found that Charlotte's 'sweet spot' was a bedtime bottle between 6:30 pm and 7:00 pm. We'd be sure to do a diaper change before the bottle, and then swaddle her with one arm down and one arm up. Once we got that, she was more consistently sleeping from 7:00 pm to 4:00 am. It felt like a miracle.

You might also hear the fun catchphrase, 'sleep begets sleep.' We have also found it to be true, that when our children napped well during the day, they slept well at night. We had many days when our babies took extra-long naps, and we were fearful that meant they wouldn't sleep at night. I'd stress out a little, and prepare myself for the worst, assuming that our baby would not go to sleep at a normal bedtime—and instead, keep us up all night. As it turns out, long naps make little difference when they are newborns and infants. Even toddlers can get away with long naps and this will have little effect on their bedtimes.

Keeping babies on a napping routine is a good idea to help with nighttime sleep! This can also be where some of the lines between whether or not your baby is running your life get blurry. No parent wants to plan their entire day around a baby's nap schedule. But sometimes, knowing your baby can get in a good nap has to take priority. You can plan your day around naps without too much effort, going out only during their wake windows, or during a commute to different places when your baby is awake or at the end of a nap…then bring a Pack 'n Play so they can nap wherever you are!

We carted Brooklyn around with us on the weekends a lot when she was a baby. She napped in her Pack 'n Play like a pro, basically wherever we went. There was no baby ruling our social life! We then turned into homebodies when we had Charlotte because she was much harder to manage and throwing that extra kid in the mix turned us into more of a circus than a family outing. Our babysitter budget went up a lot when we had Charlotte.

If you're going to go out during the day, you may experience a car nap. A car nap, if it is not of normal length, is not necessarily restorative sleep, so it might not count as a full nap for your baby. This might mean a shift in the nap schedule to a little later in the day to try and get one more solid nap in before bedtime.

Car naps are super common, and sometimes unavoidable. After I'd already had two babies, I learned that car seat naps can be a hazard— so I feel compelled to call out that you should not let your baby sleep in a car seat unless it is positioned in one of two ways:

1. In its car seat base in your vehicle (a sleeping baby while you're actually in your car is perfectly fine!)
2. Propped up to mimic the car seat base with the straps loosened

The alternative? Don't let your baby sleep in the car seat outside of the vehicle at all.

Car seats are not designed for babies to sleep in when set anywhere other than the car seat base. There have been infant fatalities when sleeping babies are set on the floor in a car seat. It is possible for them to slip down, which causes their breathing to be prevented by the car seat straps. You can Google all about it—I once saw a news article about this very situation. Use safety precautions with car seat naps!

On the topic of hazards, you can chat with your pediatrician about the safest ways to put your baby to sleep. It seems that different swaddles and sleepsuits come in and out of recommendation routinely. It is now strictly advised that a baby only sleeps on its back. If your baby can roll themselves over, then there isn't anything you can do to prevent that. Once they are able to roll over, then you'll need to stop swaddling them!

Ultimately, the key ingredient to a good nap for your baby is also likely the key ingredient for you. What's that ingredient? They'll need to be tired! We found that a routine schedule certainly helped to get them tired when they need to be, but sometimes circumstances can change that. Say, for instance, your baby took a short nap in the car soon before their scheduled naptime. You don't want to skip the nap—because, hello silence—so, you'll need to get them to play for a while before they get a real nap. Another example is, if they took a longer morning nap than usual, you'll probably need to adjust the second nap to a little later in the day.

To keep naps consistent, you'll also want to coordinate with caregivers if your baby is in any kind of daycare. Alert them of your baby's typical naptimes, and any tricks you've found that help them sleep longer. Work with your caregivers on routines to make sure that you both understand what works best.

Sleep is the main priority when it comes to having a baby. Sleep for her, sleep for you. Sleep is the magic cure to tears and hostility. I feel like this is a really cruel time to introduce what is called the sleep regression, but it is also something you'll likely want to brace yourself for, just in case.

Maybe it's a 50/50 shot that you'll encounter a sleep regression. We only did with one child! With Brooklyn, I'd heard rumors about sleep regressions. I thought they were a myth told by parents who couldn't bear to let their children cry it out for longer than 5 minutes because we never had one.

Then we had Charlotte, and I found out I was wrong. They are real.

First, let's answer: what is a sleep regression? It is when a baby who had been sleeping well at night begins waking up frequently at night, for what appears to be no apparent reason. It is common to happen around four months, again around eight months to a year, and yet again at 18 months.

Next, we answer a more important question: How does a sleep regression happen—there has to be a real reason, right? Yes, there is! Around four months, babies start to develop more mature sleeping patterns. You've heard of 'REM cycles' in sleep. Well, that is all this is. Your baby is beginning to cycle between being awake, REM sleep and deep sleep. As they come out of deep sleep to REM sleep, they are likely to awaken more easily. Small noises could startle them. Or, they could fart or twitch and wake themselves up. What do you think happens when they do that?

They freak out.

The most important question to answer: How do you fix it? Well, that starts with understanding why your baby might be freaking out. To do this, you need to consider how you are laying your baby down to sleep.

A likely scenario is that you feed and then rock your baby to sleep. This can potentially make your baby's ability to fall asleep dependent upon eating and being rocked. It doesn't seem to be a problem as a newborn when they are expected to wake several hours at night to do just that—eat! But as your baby gets older, her belly gets bigger and she can go longer without eating. And then, the habit of eating and being rocked to sleep prevents her from learning to fall asleep on her own. She freaks out when she enters a light sleep state because the last time, she was awake, she was in your arms. Then, all of a sudden, she is in her crib! New place, not sure how she got there—enter crying baby.

I know, I know. NOT rocking your baby to sleep is basically against all the motherly instincts you have. And feeding your baby before they go to sleep needs to happen! And getting a full belly tends to make a baby sleepy anyway, so it just feels natural to rock them until they're zonked out for those sweet little cuddles. But what I'd recommend trying is putting a small activity between the feeding time and laying her in the crib. Whether it is burping, changing a diaper, or swaddling, having some small activity that will wake them up just enough to have some recognition of being in the crib before falling asleep.

Eventually, you'll be laying them down fairly wide awake. We crack jokes about the 'second kid' syndrome sometimes. We sold the rocking chair in Charlotte's room when she was only nine months old. Obviously, by that time, we were certainly not concerned about rocking her to sleep! Around seven or eight months, we had even started letting her drink the nighttime bottle in a bouncer chair downstairs, so we had completely removed the association of feeding or rocking in her room. Her room and crib were only for sleep! (Of course, that came back to bite us a little when she got the flu a few months later and no chair to rock her at night when she needed comfort, so maybe you don't want to go that far.)

The second part of the sleep training equation is what you do if they do wake up at night. That is, if they wake up before you expect they are hungry. Oftentimes, our instinct is just that—baby wakes up, so she must be hungry! But maybe, that isn't the case.

- Try letting her cry for a little bit, as long as you feel comfortable. Oftentimes, a baby that has been sleeping well will be able to cry for only five minutes or so and then go back to sleep.
- Could her environment have woken her up? Is there hot or cold air blowing at her crib? Does she need to be re-swaddled and calmed down?
- Understand whether she should be hungry or not. Did she eat well earlier in the day? What might have caused her to not eat as well?

Remember, though, if your baby is very young, then waking up to eat—or for any other reason—is normal!

If you get to the end of that short list and realize she probably is hungry, think about why. Is it because she has started a pattern of waking up at night, and you've been feeding her? She might be getting more calories at night than she needs, causing her to under eat during the day and then wake up at night because she's hungry...and you'll begin to see the perpetuated cycle of the sleep regression. Although it can be impossible at times to get a baby to eat if she doesn't want to, it is important to get them their caloric needs during the day, so that a sleep regression can possibly be avoided!

The younger you start the habit of letting them fall asleep, the better off you could be. I say could, because babies are all still mystifying creatures, and even the best sleep practices sometimes can't fight a sleep regression. If you're finding yourself in this situation, you can either be miserable or you can seek help. There are some good baby sleep courses you can find online! It could very well be worth your while, so you feel less miserable.

A friend once told us something they found with their first baby, which was that you'll almost never have two bad nights in a row. I found this to generally be true—usually, a really rough night of sleep was followed up with a moderately-okay one. Sleep regressions are unpredictable, and there is not much you as a parent can do to prevent them. It is all a part of your baby maturing and learning how to sleep!

While we did have sleep regressions with Charlotte, we worked our way through them with the points below. Her regressions were never consistent enough to warrant retaining outside help, but I encouraged many friends to seek out courses or professional guidance because losing sleep is the hardest part about raising a baby!

Here are some things that worked for us, which may help you get your baby to sleep. Like all things in this book, this was my experience. My experience might work for you, or it might not. Or, you might not agree with something we did! Not all parents are a fan of crying it out. I expect this and encourage you to try different things to understand what works for you. Every family is different for a reason!

Loud white noise Some babies like it really loud. Charlotte needed a nap so bad one day, but she just refused to sleep. So, to drown out the noise, Kyle vacuumed, and I made a creamy cashew dip in the food processor. Three minutes later, she was out and slept for an hour.

Experiment with swaddles and sleepsuits We used the Velcro ones because I definitely don't have time to learn how to swaddle from a blanket or worry about my baby busting out because I was tired, too, and did a half-ass job. But there are many types of easy-to-use swaddles. Some that use Velcro and some that just zip up. Eventually, we graduated to the Magic Merlin's sleepsuit which worked like a charm for both our babies.

Make sure they have a full belly Consistent eating during the day will help make sure your baby has all of her caloric needs. We would do a dinner bottle and a big nighttime bottle to top them off! Another trick—once we got approved from our pediatrician to start feeding our babies rice cereal, we dumped a little of that in their bottles, too, making sure they were nice and full for bedtime.

Check the environment. Does the room get too hot or too cold? Is your baby laying under a vent that might wake her up when the AC turns on? We put a space heater in Charlotte's room when she was young, because her room was chronically cold, and that seemed to help her from waking up with little icicle fists.

Crying it out Probably the hardest one for most parents. Either you can't bear to hear your baby cry for so long, or you can actually hear your baby cry from anywhere in your own house without even using a monitor, so it keeps you awake anyway. There are different ways to do this, but we found that usually, our babies would go back to sleep for at least a couple of hours if we let them cry 20-30 minutes. This is also good to help babies start to self-soothe.

9 THINGS WILL HAPPEN THAT SCARE YOU

Perhaps the chapter no one wants to read, or think about, ever. But it's important to address it head-on because this is life. You are a mother now. And things will happen that scare you.

My girlfriends and I organized a moms-only get together one night around Christmas. It was the first time in years that we did something together where it was just us—no kids or husbands! We made dinner, had drinks, and watched a movie. It was super relaxing and really fun to have girl-time on that level again.

We spent a lot of time talking. Much of the dialogue referenced the fear we harvest about things that might happen to our families. It was ironic that we had blocked off an entire afternoon and night just for ourselves, to let loose and have fun, and then we spent the first several hours talking about the most morbid things that weighed heavily on our minds. Stories about kids passing away unexpectedly and stupid things we have done with our children that could have had a worse ending than what actually happened.

It was morbid, but also, strangely cathartic. Things will happen in your own life that scare you. Things will happen in other people's lives that might scare you even more. But just know that if you are constantly thinking about all the bad things that could happen, well, all the other moms are, too. You aren't alone in envisioning your own worst nightmare.

So, what can we do about that? We can't just live our whole maternal lives worrying about the worst things that can happen. We can't overshadow our little one's childhood because we're scared that they might get injured—or something worse. There are too many circumstances out of our control, and too many situations we cannot even see.

One of my girlfriends said, 'All I know is that if I did everything I could to prevent something from happening to my child, then I'd find a way to accept the situation.'

And that is all you can do! You are a great mother, and you love your child, and you're doing everything you can to keep that child safe. You are. I promise. Instead of worrying about things that might go wrong, trust that you're doing all you can, and enjoy the calm that this can bring to your life.

When you become a mother, irrational fear can creep into just about every situation. I was terrified of Brooklyn's soft spot until she was about one. Always careful not to touch it, I would freak out if her headband snapped too hard on the top of her head. I would vividly imagine something puncturing her soft spot. When we'd go back to Indiana and stay with Kyle's parents, Brooklyn would inevitably play in their family room. They have these end tables with glass tops and black metal legs. The legs have pointy, metal decorative leaves on them, and some of them curve downward. It looks like the perfect angle for a baby to accidentally pull up on and have a metal leaf run straight through her head.

I feel so ridiculous admitting that story. I'm weird and have irrational fears, but I guarantee you that I am not the only one who has inadvertently thought about these very unlikely, strange scenarios. I made a comment about those tables being unsafe once, and Kyle's dad simply said, 'Well, we've had four grandbabies here through the years and they're all okay.'

Yep. They're all okay, and Brooklyn was okay, and I needed to STFU because my motherly imagination was irrationally running wild.

Speaking of your baby's soft spot, I'll prepare you for another irrational fear that something might be wrong. When Brooklyn was a couple of weeks old, I noticed that the soft spot on her head would pulsate. Noticeably, the top of her head would pulse up and down. As a first-time mom, I automatically assumed something was wrong, though I had no idea what—like her brain was going to grow outside her skull? Afraid there was just one, thin layer of skin covering the top of her brain that a shiny, decorative leave might puncture? I am a woman educated in science and this should not have been a thought that crossed my mind. (Shaking my own head at myself right now.) That pulsating is creepy and weird to watch, but also totally normal and nowhere near life-threatening, as I learned after asking my mother-in-law about it as they were there to help out. (At least I didn't go to the doctor for that one.) The soft spot is basically just a membrane, and your baby's head will sometimes pulse with the beat of their heart. Babies are weird. Irrational Mom fears are weirder.

You might not think you're doing everything right, because, with your first child, you probably won't know what the hell you're doing at all. I mean that quite literally. Just like most things in life you do for the first time, you might have to wing it a little. But ya know what? They call it a maternal instinct for a reason. Most things you try might not be the best or easiest way, but it'll be good enough. You'll figure it out.

And when in doubt, call someone to ask. Because that's part of figuring it out.

Trust yourself that you'll keep your child safe.

Also allow yourself grace if there is a mistake. Inevitably, you'll do things with your children that scare you. Or you might hear stories about other parents making mistakes, like not strapping their baby into the seat of their baby swing, and hearing their baby fly out. That actually happened to someone I know. Fair warning: if there is a safety strap on something, it's there for a reason. Just use it.

There are a few stories that come to mind about things I personally did that scared me.

The first one I remember happened when Brooklyn was about a month old. We were practicing tummy time in her room. She was starting to get tired and rest her head on the ground, so I went to flip her onto her back. But I was lazy about it, and didn't really lift her up, so I accidentally laid her down with one arm completely bent backward, under her back, in a way an arm shouldn't be bending. She started bawling and I automatically assumed I had dislocated her arm.

But I did not! Babies are strangely malleable and can survive even after rolling off a diaper changing table (another mom-friend story).

Another incident when Brooklyn was one month was when her car seat had gotten unbuckled in the back seat, and I didn't know. I was driving some people in my car along with Brooklyn, and the person in the back seat somehow accidentally unbuckled the seatbelt in the middle that secured Brooklyn's car seat, instead of their own, when exiting the car. At least, I assume that's what happened. A few days later, after I had already driven with her several more times, I realized that her car seat wasn't even strapped into the back seat at all. Had we gotten into an accident; it could have been really bad.

That was a hypothetical situation that thankfully did not happen. But had it occurred, I wouldn't have known there was an issue, and therefore something I could not have held myself to blame.

The next one is embarrassing. Brooklyn was maybe five months old, and I was giving her a bath. She had graduated into a blow-up tub that was in the bottom of our shower. She had just started to get really fun in the tub, playing with toys, although she couldn't fully sit up yet. The tub was small enough that she could lean against the back, with her legs pushed against the front, to force herself to sit.

I had my phone with me because I was taking some pictures. And then, I got a text message. Which I checked. And in those few seconds between taking my eyes off Brooklyn, who seemed perfectly fine in the tub, and looking at my phone, she slipped down and her head submerged in the water. I had caught her instantly, and she couldn't have been under for more than a second (and babies get thrown into the water during swim classes, so I've been told it's an instinct that they don't breathe), but it was a silly mistake for me to get distracted, and it scared me for a long time. Mistakes happen, and we have to give ourselves grace for that.

This last one...funnier than anything. Not even a mistake, but it mortified me when it happened. It's one of those random things that will happen, that might scare you.

I was getting ready for work, and Brooklyn was sitting on my bathroom floor, playing with some toys. She had crawled around a little, and I assumed she was playing with clothes or some other random item that was more interesting than the toys we actually bought her. But then I turned around. She had her back to me, and I realized it looked like she was hitting the floor. Not that it was unusual, but something made me pay attention.

I came into her vision, and she looked up at me with a huge smile on her face...and a slobbery leg of a cockroach stuck to her chin. The 'toy' she was playing with in front of her was actually a dying cockroach.

It's gross. I felt like I should never tell anyone this happened. Maybe I shouldn't have written it in this book...but ya know what? Kids are gonna play with bugs, and some of us have homes with cockroaches even if the house itself is clean. I couldn't have done anything to prevent that from happening. Yes, it's disgusting. And I was maybe a little scared she might have picked up some ancient disease carried around on the back of a cockroach. But she was just fine, even if I was scarred for life.

These weird things happen, and it can happen to any mom, so you just need to pick up and move on.

Weird things, hurtful things, and maybe just some bad things will happen to your kids. It's the terrifying reality of life. You can't protect them from everything, because it's physically impossible. But you'll do your best, that is all you can do!

10 YOUR BODY WILL CHANGE

After having a baby, it seems pretty obvious that your body will change. Not only that it should somewhat 'normalize' after having given birth to a human, but remember, you also just gave BIRTH to a human. When you think about it, there is no possible way your body could ever be exactly the same. Your body went through something it had never experienced, so of course, there are going to be incredible changes to your body.

Did you know that 'incredible' can not only mean 'amazing' or 'astonishing,' but also 'unbelievable' or 'absurd'? In its definition regarding body change, we're going to refer to the latter.

The most in-your-face body change is going to be weight gain. It's a necessary process for you to grow a healthy baby. I doubt we'll ever really know why some women gain much more weight than others (assuming pregnancy isn't used as an excuse to eat fast food every day). My own observations show that petite women tend to gain much more weight than average women, and also that the amount of weight you gain doesn't necessarily mean it will take you more or less time to lose it. Sometimes, it magically falls off. It's quite a peculiar mystery, this pregnancy weight.

I do wholeheartedly believe that if you eat healthily and you maintain moderate activity that you shouldn't have much of a problem getting close to your pre-pregnancy weight again, within a reasonable timeframe. Reasonable being maybe a year or so since it did take almost one year to put it on. Just like any type of weight loss, if you aren't eating healthy and you are not active, that extra weight isn't really going to go anywhere. A lot of immediate weight you'll shed is fluids that will be metabolized by your body naturally, but the actual fat you put on will likely need some additional effort.

My first pregnancy weight gain came in around 35 pounds. It was at the upper end of the healthy range and honestly, I had to be okay with it because there really wasn't anything that I could do about it. I wrongly assumed, though, what those 35 pounds were and how they were going to be shed.

Logic would tell you that a simple math equation could calculate how much weight you'd still carry after you give birth to an 8-pound, 4-ounce baby.

	35-pound weight gain
-	8.25 pounds of baby
-	1.5 pounds of placenta
-	1.8 pounds of amniotic fluid

23.45 pounds

You'd think I would have lost at least 12-13 pounds after delivery, when it's all said and done.

After birth, staying two days in the hospital and then a full day at home, I stepped on the scale. Do you know how much weight I lost?

6 pounds.

How in the living hell was it possible that I only lost 6 pounds?! I birthed an 8-pound baby! This was not logical. It was nonsensical.

I didn't look like I had lost weight, either. Why didn't anybody tell me I'd still look 7 months pregnant after having a baby? I was so confused, and I was frustrated. And I did not know it was completely normal.

Welcome to pregnancy weight gain.

I was so irritated with my looks in those first few weeks. No clothes felt comfortable. I was not really losing weight, but I was also unable to exercise until I was cleared by my doctor at one-month post-partum. And I was eating like CRAZY. I was still breastfeeding and pumping for about 6 weeks, and that hunger was unreal. Breastfeeding and pumping did not make my weight fall off, and I don't know many women who are able to rely on that as their sole means of weight-loss, even though it is touted as a benefit to breastfeeding.

I was hard on myself, especially as I walked around the house after a 1 am feeding, scowling as my water-retaining ankles jiggled like a cup of Jell-O.

I have a picture of myself, holding Brooklyn, on my very first Mother's Day. It was one week after she was born. At that point, it was hard for me to see myself for what I actually was—a proud and excited first-time mom, with a baby girl who would grow to love me more than anyone else. I looked at that picture with distain. I didn't want anyone to see it. I had a difficult time with negative self-talk. (Although I could not accept myself at that point in my life, I luckily no longer feel that way.)

I desperately wanted to ditch my maternity clothes, but they were still the only thing that fit me. I actually wore maternity jeans for a good six months after having Brooklyn, before I went out and bought real jeans in larger sizes. It took me over a year to comfortably fit into most of my clothes pre-pregnancy, but several things were just never going to fit again. Although you can eventually get back to your pre-pregnancy weight, you'll likely experience that the fat you do carry is proportioned much differently than it was before.

Although I have always had cellulite on my legs, they were always pretty skinny. But after having babies, I carry so much more weight in my hips and outer thighs. I credit a lot of this to muscle deterioration. The muscle definition in my legs completely disappeared. It'll take a long time to get back. I don't doubt that with enough work I can reshape my legs the way I want them, but with two kids at home, working out every single day is impeccably more difficult.

Nor do I want to dedicate so much time to working out, if we're being honest. Just as your body changes, your priorities change, too. And it helps if you can give yourself some grace and realize that your body does not define you. For someone who has struggled with body image their entire life, I know acceptance of yourself is one of the hardest things you can do. I've come to be okay with the way I look because ultimately, I have a healthy body that can get stronger day by day. I choose to work out when I want to, and I do my best to schedule it in during the day. If I've hit my goal of 3 workouts a week, then I'm gonna opt for 'mommy cuddles' with my toddler who needs some lovin,' even if it means watching Moana for the 1500th time.

Weight gain isn't the only body change you might experience. While every woman is different in how their body changes, this is what happened to me.

My boobs became the laughingstock of my 25-year-old self. I did expect that my boobs would change. My mom friends were sure to inform me of this once I became pregnant. It's hard to imagine what a 'flat pancake' or 'deflated balloon' of a boob looks like unless you see one, and it's a real shocker when the first time you see one is in the mirror after you've given up breastfeeding. Your boobs will look just like a sad, deflated balloon that is still attached to its ribbon, hanging off a mailbox after a whirlwind birthday party. Your floppy-balloon-boobs will be the remains of a party you threw but didn't get to enjoy because you were too busy making sure everyone else had fun.

While the topic of breast implants has come up in discussion with my husband, it was not because he wants me to get one. Luckily, my man still likes my floppy little breasts. Your man will, too, as long as you let him play with them. (Which you should, it'll probably make you feel better about your life in general.) I am much too terrified of elective surgery to ever commit to getting a boob job, so, for now, I will rely on a properly sized push-up bra (which took me forever to find, by the way) to make me look less like my boobs are hanging half-way down my stomach. Although I am not sure I'd ever get a boob job, I can now, 100% understand why any woman would choose to do it.

Likely in part because my boobs are less on my chest and more hanging off my chest, my actual chest feels much wider. It's difficult to describe. It feels broad. Any kind of low-cut blouse or strapless swimsuit makes me feel like a tween trying to look like a grown-up. It's weird and this is a large reason why I ditched a lot of clothing after having a baby. I eventually lost the weight, but my body was just shaped differently.

Speaking of things getting wider…let's talk about those hips. I've always had a wider frame, with broad shoulders and wide hip bones. I never actually measured, but after having Brooklyn, I'm certain that my hips grew by inches. After reaching my pre-pregnancy weight the first time around, I was still in jean sizes larger than before. Once I had Charlotte, I started wearing a hip contraction belt almost every day. Again, I never measured because I really hate judging my body off a number, but it made a very noticeable difference, and I'm once again in the same size jeans as my pre-pregnancy self.

There are some pregnancy symptoms that you might have benefited from…but they might not last. For example, during pregnancy, your hair gets really thick. It might not always look good—mine didn't— but it just stops falling out. But between 4-and 6-months post-partum, the hair that didn't fall out during pregnancy starts coming out in clumps. It's a little scary, and you might think for a while that you're going bald because it starts getting really thin around your forehead. Don't worry! You won't get bald. It will grow back. Which is almost as annoying because you're then dealing with baby hairs around the front of your face for a year or two, depending on how fast your hair grows. It's even worse if it grows back gray, like almost all of mine did after baby number two. Gray hairs are stiffer, and they tend to grow straight up. Exploding out of my scalp. This is when hairspray becomes a close companion.

It won't just be the hair on your head that falls out. I wish I could tell you it'd fall out in inconvenient places like your armpits or legs.

Obviously not, though, because nothing about recovering from pregnancy is convenient. Instead, your eyelashes might also fall out. Please take a deep breath. It might not happen to you, but if it does, trust that these will grow back, too. There may be a time, though, when mascara just looks weird because your lashes are spaced out way more than normal. If I were any good at make-up, I might have become addicted to fake lashes at this time in my life.

After pregnancy, I also started to have different types of skin issues. I've always had rosacea, but it got worse during and after pregnancy. Breakouts and persistent redness became more common. Or course, it is possible this may have happened with age. I would speculate it was caused in part by the influx of hormones, making all kinds of changes inside and outside of my body. Some women experience the opposite, and their skin completely clears up. I wasn't so lucky and still struggle with it, more than a year after giving birth.

Physical appearance is not the only effect of pregnancy. You might find that your immune system goes to complete shit. It wasn't so bad when I was on maternity leave, but almost as soon as our babies started daycare, we'd have new germs in the house. My body was still in recovery mode, and the baby had a brand-new immune system, so inevitably baby would get a cold, and I would be down with a cold as well. I had a cold once a month for probably four months after Brooklyn started daycare. I also got the flu for the first time in years. It's something that does get better, as your body recovers and you can keep yourself healthy, but the struggle is definitely real.

Ultimately, probably the worst effect I had from pregnancy was an abdominal separation, known as diastasis recti. I hadn't even learned about what diastasis was until after I had Brooklyn and realized in hindsight that it definitely happened to me. Essentially, due to the growing size of your belly, the muscles in your abdomen begin to separate, starting near your belly button. It's quite common, but from what I understand after speaking to several physical therapists, it goes undiagnosed, and many doctors don't preemptively suggest therapy. I noticed I had it because when I sat up, my stomach would get a weird peak in the middle of it instead of staying round. The real effects of it were felt after my baby was born.

It's something you should definitely discuss with your doctor, or seek help from a physical therapist, especially so you understand how to properly recover. Once you're cleared to work out again, it's important to make sure you start easy enough for your core to keep up and build back its strength. There are tons of resources online for this, and you can also chat with your doctor to test out physical therapy. With Brooklyn, I made the mistake of jumping back into workouts that I wasn't ready for, and I had trained improperly. I actually ended up in physical therapy as a result of it because I developed persistent knee pain, which was made worse by pursuing physical activity. In physical therapy, I started small, retraining my core the proper way. Eventually, my core was strong again, and the knee pain subsided. Ironically, I got pregnant again right after my knee pain was gone. But the next time around, I knew how to regain my strength in the right way!

After I knew I was done having kids, I made a serious effort to try and regain control over my body. There is so much out of your control when you are pregnant. Your body just does its own thing, and you're essentially along for the ride, not knowing where you might end up.

Regaining control of my body, and weight gain specifically, wasn't actually much of an issue for me in my second pregnancy—in a mental sense. I knew going in that I was going to gain weight. I approached it with an educated, optimistic perspective, which coincidentally helped empower me to stay relatively healthy throughout those nine months. My food choices were better, in part from a dairy sensitivity I seemed to develop after having Brooklyn. Instead of surviving off pizza, grilled cheese and cheeseburgers—the true comfort foods that made up most of my diet with Brooklyn—I focused on vegetables (after my first trimester when they didn't make me gag) and tried to engage in some low-impact activity when I could. I didn't attempt harder workouts after the first trimester, because my knee pain had come back, and that kind of physical exertion was not a priority for me. Keeping up with Brooklyn as a toddler was my priority, and it proved to be enough activity for me while simultaneously growing a baby. I still put on weight, though still a healthy amount of 30 pounds instead of 35. To my surprise, I lost almost all of it by the time Charlotte was 3 months old. However, it's taken a lot longer to regain muscle.

I'd say my dedication to nutrition certainly paid off, but you also can't disregard the calm and mental clarity I had about my body changes going into it. I already knew what to expect. I demanded patience of myself to let my body do what it needed to do and trusted that after she was born, everything would be okay, no matter how long it took for the weight to drop off.

One year after having our second baby, I am in the best shape of my life. That's not going to be the case for everybody, because no two bodies are the same, and my health is something I'll continue to work on forever. But I have stayed dedicated to a mostly healthy diet, working out when I can, and keeping a good attitude about my body image. I still have good days and bad days, just like before, but I do my best to put my own health at the top of my priority list.

I encourage you to find healthy habits that work for you. Keeping healthy when you have a newborn is not easy, and we're inundated with whatever is convenient to eat, and a lack of sleep. So, start small! This will help you mentally, boost your immune system, and allow you to be a healthier, happier parent to your newborn.

Don't force anything. It's why you should start small. You won't reclaim your body overnight, and it might not even happen within a few weeks. Don't succumb to a negative attitude if you feel like your progress is too slow. Don't force a hard workout before you're ready, just because you want to see results. Take your time and give yourself grace.

Also, remember that you don't need to fit into your pre-pregnancy clothes. They might not fit the same regardless of how much time passes! I required almost a whole new wardrobe because nothing fit the same. Find clothing that you feel good in and accept you may still be in maternity clothes for some time. (It also helps that high-rise jeans are back in style because those suckers hide everything.)

Most importantly, when you are in your postpartum journey, don't forget to be kind to yourself.

Speak to yourself like you are your own friend.

Be with people that support you, and don't compare your journey to anyone else's. Maybe your body changes won't be an issue for you—and I hope that is true!

10 YOUR HAPPILY HECTIC-EVER-AFTER

I used to blog about healthy living. I'm kind of half-ass about it now (more like quarter-ass, or ass-falling-off-the-seat) but I do show up on Instagram semi-regularly to post about food, staying healthy and eco-friendly living suggestions. You know, the things I am passionate about that I can spew all over the few followers of my personal IG account. The blog has slowly died and turned into influencing my friends to make themselves and the Earth better for everyone.

We do weekend food prep, cook healthy meals, and work out regularly because it is required if we want to live a long and healthy life. It is also required if you want to feel good. Not just feel good superficially—like, oh-I'm-so-skinny—but to have energy, sleep well, (hopefully) have clearer skin, and not have irregular bowel movements (you all know what I'm talking about here, remember you have to get used to talking about poop a lot in your life now).

I also have a full-time job in marketing technology and advertising which is a shit show of an industry and can tend to drive you crazy. Like, literally go bat shit about once a month. Advertising is an urgent industry, and when deadlines aren't met, everyone's ass is on the line. It's what can make the industry a pain in the ass. Everything about it is URGENT. Now, now, now.

You know what else is urgent? Your kids. Snacks and diapers and baths and playtime and also cuddle time. It's all a necessary and required part of parenting, and it is also sometimes a pain in the ass. Some of these things are obvious necessities. Food and diaper changes, because your kids need nourishment and cleanliness. But the playtime and the cuddles—while less obvious as a necessity—are sometimes the only things that might stop either you or your children from having a dramatic meltdown.

Every once in a while, I get people telling me I am a Super Mom. Most recently, "Tell me how TF you have time for two dogs, two adorable babies, a 24/7 job and being an Insta influencer. Teach me." My response was, "I wake up early AF, that's probably how. Also, I cried on the way to work yesterday. So, there's that."

I know this message was sent to me as a compliment, but it makes me laugh. I would not classify myself as a Super Mom. I mean, I'll admit, I am a Type A who is good at getting shit done. But I am strung out a lot of the time. I get jealous when my husband gets to do fun things for work that my job doesn't allow. And sometimes, I cry because of it, when I am at home with the children, picking up peas off the floor. I yell at my kids. I never mop my floors (I actually hire help to do things like that). I never take naps when I'm tired because dishes and laundry need to get done. Lately, I've been prioritizing the tactical things that make our days run more smoothly. I could set aside more time to play with my kids. Actually, I should do that. It's something I actively work on. But there has to be some kind of balance so that our lives don't run out of control. The balance will swing differently every day, and it will likely be different for you than it is for me.

On top of prioritizing the job, the kids, and the tactical things—I also prioritize taking care of my own health. I make exercise mandatory. I've stopped letting house chores get in the way of that, and I have to accept the fact that sometimes, chores won't get done so that I can take care of myself.

Remember that you don't need to do all the things picture perfectly. I stress myself out sometimes about what my kids are eating. It took me three years to buy regular jelly to make a PB&J for Brooklyn, because I was afraid it was too much sugar. I do food prep, but I can't always get the littles to eat vegetables, so they have macaroni and cheese and chicken nuggets for dinner 3 nights a week. And that is completely okay! Is it 'picture perfect?' To some, maybe not. But it's perfect in my house. I'd rather get them to eat anything at all than reenact Battle of the Broccoli every night.

There is no teaching this beautiful mess of a life. Some things will be easier than other things. And everyone does things differently based on what they want to prioritize.

A lot of what you prioritize might come down to convenience. We food prep because we prioritize our health, but we also carefully budget our money to pay off student loans and save for the future. There are lots of other ways to feed yourself and your family that may be more convenient, like healthy pre-made meals you can pick-up or have delivered. Those also cost more money. You might find yourself in a position where you can and want to buy more prepared meals or provide more foods from the freezer section. (I mean, we keep chicken nuggets and microwave pizzas in stock at all times). Those are decisions you are allowed to make. No one but you get to decide how you parent or live your life. That includes how you feed yourself and your kids.

I also probably stress over things I shouldn't, like keeping up with dishes and laundry. I know my husband would tell me I'm a fool for letting it 'worry me.' I wouldn't necessarily go that far, but I do get peace from having a clean sink and countertop and an empty laundry bin. But there are also nights when I let myself slow down and just enjoy family time because that's a priority, too. I don't know if I'll ever find the right balance. It probably won't be until my kids are old enough to load the dishwasher themselves.

Isn't balance like an ever-changing thing, anyway? There will always be new routines, goals, passions, needs. It's one of those elusive dreams we're always striving towards, but we don't even know what it looks like. It's never perfect, and as long as you're mindfully working on it—keeping yourself content and focused on what is most important in the moment—that is good enough.

There will always be unexpected frustrations, too, and you've gotta do your best to roll through it. Like when your 8-month-old baby decides that, all of a sudden, she hates being in the car seat and screams bloody murder when you strap her in, and it doesn't stop until you arrive home and take her out again.

There will be frustrating moments. And they can be overwhelming.

You might live a large percentage of your life in what I call 'the overwhelm.' There are days when I sit in the daycare parking lot at 6 pm with emotional turmoil. It's a mixture of excitement, fear and dread. I have to pick them up, and I want to see them, but I have no idea what kind of mood they'll be in, or what they're going to whine about, or whether they're going to let me set them down without crying. 'The overwhelm' is the unexplainable feeling of stress mixed with anxiety that is actually explained by all the craziness in your life. The job. The kids. The dishes. The laundry. The dogs. Everything else that's calling your name. It can get the best of you if you don't take at least a little time for yourself once in a while to reset.

The odd thing is that you will feel 'the overwhelm' when your kids are awake, and you're at home trying to put dinner on the table. Half the family crying about something. You have a kid pulling on your leg as you're trying to boil water for pasta. The dogs still have to get fed. You're then in a hurried frenzy as you bathe, wrangle, change and put the children to bed so you can sit down and do something for yourself for the first time all day.

Finally, the kids are asleep, and the kitchen is clean. It's quiet. Which is what you've been wanting since you got home! But instead of a blissful sense of calm, you might feel something completely different and unexpected.

Many days, I will feel 'the overwhelm' while my children are awake. And sometimes, it is followed by guilt after they go to sleep.

Am I spending enough time with my children?

Am I a bad mom for feeling overwhelmed when they cry?

Why do I get annoyed when Charlotte pulls on my legs, crying to be held? Should I be wanting to soak up as many cuddles with her as I can? Isn't that how a good mom is supposed to feel?

How is it even possible to feel guilty about not spending time with the people that are also overwhelming you in the same night?

It makes no sense, and it falls into that 90% category of parenting that is the confusing, beautiful mess of a life with children. That messy 90% of parenting is filled with fighting battles with your children about finishing chicken nuggets or going pee in the potty. But the messy part is also about fighting internal struggles like wondering whether you're showing your children enough love.

JUST so you know...there is absolutely, without a doubt, no question about whether your children know you love them. Trust me. They know. And you are doing more than enough to show them your love. You show up, every day, and you're there for them. That is enough!

Much of 'the overwhelm' you'll experience is being fearful or anxious for what is coming next. Like my daycare parking lot drama, it's anticipating that once you pick up the kids, the rest of the night will go poorly. In these situations, the only thing to do is adjust your mindset.

Instead of expecting the worst out of your children, own where you are at in this stage of life, and go into any situation that involves your kids with the anticipation that everything will be just fine. I know, easier said than done. To support this theory, here is a quote that resonated with me on the topic.

If you are depressed, you are living in the past. If you are anxious, you are living in the future. If you are at peace, you are living in the present." — Lao Tzu

Can we agree that this is 100% true, and can actually apply to almost any situation in life? I make myself anxious sometimes about how badly my kids are going to behave before they are even misbehaving. And, maybe, they won't even misbehave at all! The result is that I've put myself in that crappy mood for no reason. That bad mood makes it harder to actually enjoy the present and watch them play together, let alone play along with them. And if they do misbehave, so be it! It's safe to assume that nothing will likely go according to plan, and the only time that's a bad thing is if you were expecting perfection. You could plan out a weekend trip to brunch and the zoo. You might have good manners and get smiling pictures. But chances are you'll be asking for the check early at the restaurant, and then carry your child who is now scared of animals all the way around the zoo. Either situation is okay, and the latter is probably considered normal. You'll be able to savor smaller memories between the arduous moments.

It's a good idea to keep your head in the present, enjoy the moments, own them, and just let yourself be happy. You can't control your kids' actions or emotions, but you can control your attitude and make the best of whatever situation you encounter.

Of course, there will be times when you're fed up. You're over it. You can't take another minute. You'll threaten to lock yourself in the bedroom and never come out...and you might do it.

And it's allowed. At least for like 5-10 minutes.

Every mom feels this way sometimes. Raising children is a challenge. Anything worth having doesn't come easy and that includes your children. I remember my mom storming outside once when we were young. She went and threw sticks against the garage wall. I don't remember why but I do remember thinking she'd gone bat shit crazy. Now, with two kids, I wish I had more sticks in my yard.

I'm sure you'll find your own version of that. For me, sometimes it's screaming out loud, even if my children are present. I do feel bad, but it brings us all back to reality. It has occasionally gotten them to stop their whining. On the more traditional and recommended stress-relief side, I'll also journal, listen to music, or just ask Kyle to take over for 5 minutes so I can 'freaking go to the bathroom in peace.'

After you have kids, there may be slivers of moments when you'll wonder why the hell you did this to your life. It sounds so awful to say aloud...but I have often wondered what my life would be like without my kids. What would I do with all my free time? What would it be like to sleep in on the weekend? Or have free rein to go to happy hour after work—or even work late without having to worry about who is picking up the kids? Would I be incredibly successful, or will I just have watched every vampire show on Netflix?

It's okay to wonder things like that, too. You know, as long as you don't actually abandon your kids at the fire station someday in search of that dreamlife. Which you won't do, because you're not a monster, and almost immediately after you let your mind wander there, you'll then wonder what the hell you'd be doing without them and how boring life would be if they weren't in it. (Insert binge-watching vampire shows.)

Through all the frustrated tears, upset feelings, and jealousy of not being the parent who gets to do less of the parenting, good things will happen. You'll find some balance with your spouse, splitting chores and childcare responsibilities. The kids will have good days. You'll find time to laugh, play and just be together.

Being a parent is hard, and can bring the overwhelm, but being a spouse, and managing the responsibilities of your children, can bring the overwhelm, too.

Marriage, in general, is hard work. It sounds like such a cliché thing to say, but the truth is that in order to build a life with someone else that is truly great, there is a lot of communication and compromise that needs to happen. You don't stay the same people that were newlyweds forever, and as people evolve, you need to talk about it. You'll have different wants and needs, and when you have kids its more important than ever to express them.

I can say with absolute certainty that we have a rock-solid marriage. It's taken years to be effective communicators, and there are definitely times when we struggle emotionally with balance between ourselves and our children. The work on our marriage has proven to be much harder once we had one, then two children interjected into the mix. There is no longer freedom to stay up late and sleep in. Or go make plans whenever you want. Or make a 'quick run' to the grocery store. We have an agreed upon schedule for working out each day. And yes, we know that we've made these sacrifices because we love our children to freaking pieces. There's no hiding all of the strung-out mornings, spit-up covered shirts, greasy messy buns and bickering about who had to change the poopy diaper that come along with it. It's not always pretty, and you need to put in the effort to make your life with children work for both of you.

Your marriage will look different than anyone else's marriage. You might have different struggles, different fights, and a different balance for how your family will function. Try not to compare another couple's balance to your own, because it might not work for you.

We know that comparison is no good.

When Brooklyn was born, a friend recommended following a bunch of popular Moms on social media—mostly for the fashion suggestions for both mom and baby, but also just because they're fun women with good advice. There isn't much to do on maternity leave between feeding, changing diapers and 'sleeping when the baby sleeps,' so naturally, my social media habits dramatically worsened.

You might compare your own marriage to your friend's, who might seem to have a better routine than you. But comparing your life to anything you see online is a very dangerous trap.

I'd see all these pictures of moms, posing with their smiling kids and beautiful babies. The kids were dressed better than me most days of the week. And don't forget the matching outfits! Not even like, oh my family is all wearing the same color scheme, aren't we cute? I mean the mom and daughter outfit match that looks both incredibly cute and deeply desirable.

To this day, I can't tell you how many times I've thought, "Should I be the mom who has matching outfits with her daughter? Why can't I get her to only choose black, gray and other neutral colors from her closet like me instead of wanting to wear all this bright pink, sparkly unicorn shit all the time? My family should be more glamorous like this."

Then I pick my face up off of my phone, look around into the real world, and realize that most mothers who go anywhere in public don't have matching outfits with their children. Why? Because they're probably a little pricey, and their daughters (like mine) want to wear bright pink and purple garbage that makes you cringe. Oh, and ALSO a child's clothes are covered in either drool, snot, food or dirt 90% of the time that they are awake.

Moms on social media will have the best toys, that happen to actually match their home decor. They'll have perfectly organized systems to store the toys, and conveniently only one toy comes out of the closet at a time, like their children are trained to put a toy away when they're done with it.

Moms on social media will have trendy diaper bags and cute hairdos and field trips where everyone in the family is having fun.

There is no family with a reality like this.

Almost anything you see on social media is staged, with a lot of planning that goes into the ideas and aesthetic of the image. Why? Because that is their job! It is how they make money. Social media is the new magazine subscription, only its free to anyone who wants to follow.

I am not saying that everything you see on social media is bad. But it is unhealthy if you let it influence you to the point of feeling like you're a bad mother or if it makes you think that your family doesn't have enough.

I've repositioned my outlook on social media. We all know it for what it is—a place for many people to curate pretty pictures and be a self-proclaimed expert. It is not a representation of anyone's life, and we should all know and own this by now.

So, don't compare your life to anyone else's. We've got that down.

You know what else you shouldn't do? Compare your baby to other babies. All babies roll, crawl, walk and talk on their own time. Some do it much faster than others. Some much slower. Siblings will hit milestones at different ages, even though the parenting and skill-building lessons were exactly the same. You should also not assume that something is wrong if your baby hasn't rolled over yet, even though the app on your smartphone says she should be rolling by now.

Oh gosh, the apps. Have I talked about apps yet? (Yes, we covered a whole section on those.) Apps can be helpful, but they can also be synonymous to googling what it means when you have a weird rash on your arm. You have a tiny rash, but then all of a sudden, you're dying and have cancer. The app says your baby should roll both ways, but that doesn't mean your baby is developmentally challenged because she can't yet roll from back to front. Maybe your baby has a bigger and heavier head than most babies, or chunkier legs that are harder to twist around. Or maybe your baby is carried around all over the place and doesn't want to roll. (All reasons why we thought Charlotte didn't roll over until she was 6 months, including speculation around whether she was just lazy.) That doesn't mean she won't do it on her own time.

Know that without the matching outfits and perfectly planned weekends at the zoo with club sandwiches cut into star shapes, you are doing enough. Comparisons will only drag you down a depressing rabbit hole. Your kid might only like peanut butter and jelly sandwiches, or mac 'n cheese and breakfast bars. Your kid might only want to wear the same shirt over and over again, and it might look a size too small, but you don't have it in you to have the argument every day.

What you own is enough, what you can provide is enough, and your love is enough. Your baby will grow and act differently than other babies, and that is okay, too. The comparison trap is an evil thing and it is easy to get lost there. So, just don't do it.

Let's be less depressing for a minute. In the midst of your hectic-ever-after, there is good stuff.

There are so many happy moments, and sometimes the intensity of love that you'll feel will make your heart explode like the Grinch. Your heart growing four sizes in one day is literally the thing that defines parenthood. It is an indefinable love which defies all logic and reason.

You would never keep any other person in your life who screamed bloody murder at 3 am or threw mac 'n cheese on the floor because it wasn't supposed to have cheese in it. Motherhood is a kind of love that is impossible to describe and might feel impossible to live without once you've had it.

I remember seeing one of my best friends with her baby when he was roughly 9 months old, just before we had Brooklyn. We were standing around in their kitchen and she was about to get him ready for bed. And she just kept giving him kisses. Like, maybe 10 to 20 kisses on the cheeks. I explicitly remember thinking how weird that was…isn't one enough? Why do you want to keep kissing your baby on the cheeks? I mean, yea, they are super squishy and he's adorable but, come on! It's borderline OCD.

For a reason I cannot explain, that must defy all logic, I now do the same thing. And it brings me SO much joy. Just something about planting your lips on a soft, squishy baby cheek. And their smiles and giggles after you do it. My heart is sparkling just thinking about it.

The kind of love you have for your children is conflicted with guilt and anger and sometimes rage, sometimes despair, but then again, more love than anything else.

Your life is going to change forever—in good ways and uncomfortable ways. I don't just mean in gross or weird ways, like the amount of times you'll change a diaper, get covered in puke or have to pick your child's nose—although weird and gross *is* true when it comes to parenting.

(Here comes the poop talk again, because that is definitely gross.)

You'll talk about your baby's poop schedule at the pediatrician, challenge yourself to find the most efficient way to change your child out of a onesie that is filled with a leaky blowout, or chat with your friends about getting your toddler to poop on a toilet. You'll ask your husband why he takes so many 30 minutes 'poops' now, so many that you might think he has developed either irritable bowel syndrome, or he has a serious mobile poker gambling habit, because *obviously* he is not just pooping in there. And you won't even be siloed to talking about your own family's poop. You might have a new-mom friend texting you pictures of their kids' poop to see if it looks normal or not. (This happened to me once.)

Your life is going to change, and I also don't just mean in silly ways like staring at the baby monitor for five minutes straight because you're 'not quite sure' if she's breathing. You'll put elves on shelves at Christmas time, unintentionally memorize a Disney movie and accidentally start singing it at work, or make animal noises and faces to get your baby to giggle.

Speaking of silly things, you might come up with the most ridiculous nicknames for your child. Seriously though, the names that have come out of my mouth are baffling. I once called Brooklyn 'my little pumpkin spice latte.' Charlotte is dubbed Charlie, and in her colic days we called her a bear, so she will forever be known as Charlie Bear. Charlie Bear, which has the same cadence as Christmas Tree, even got her own song. I made several renditions of 'O Charlie Bear' for her that I've never sung in front of anyone except Charlie Bear.

'O Charlie Bear, O Charlie Bear! How pretty are your blue eyes…'

I mean, you can understand how it would be catchy when you're home alone with a baby, right?

Your life will change as you realize how you'd rather focus on the things that actually matter in your life. The word 'priority' will officially take on an all-new meaning for you. Perhaps the word 'priority' didn't even mean a damn thing before you had kids.

Priorities will now rule your life. This can be frustrating and uncomfortable, if you let it be. You can fight it with all your being and make yourself miserable if you let yourself live in the past life of non-priorities. Wishing you could go back to more carefree days when you didn't need to pick up children from daycare and spend 2-3 hours every single night either feeding, supervising scooter-riding or block-building, bathing and fighting nighttime routines.

I have done this daydreaming of my past self. I have fought the pull of my true priorities, especially on nights when Kyle is gone and I am home by myself, listening to all their crying (why all the crying?? I wish I ever knew), wiping poopy butts, cleaning snotty noses and spooning food into both my baby and toddler's mouths between sobs because apparently hanger was passed down to them from me.

It can be easy to give in to feeling miserable and upset about the things you have to do for your children. Have you ever heard that it takes fewer muscles to smile than to frown? The same concept applies emotionally. You will drain yourself of all that is good if you give in to the misery. You'll use a lot less mental energy if you just let your new priorities make you happy. Yes, there are hard parts to parenting. Parenting is the hardest job there is. But there are also incredibly happy parts if you let yourself see them.

Let the negativity go each time you feel it coming back. Remember that if you weren't playing with your kids after work, you'd probably be doing something much less important with your life. If there are other important things you need to be doing during the time your children are awake, like cooking or working out, try to incorporate your kids into that routine. Do you know how much exercise you could get if you just ran around in the yard with your kids? If that doesn't sound fun to you, then you'll need to figure out how schedule it when they're not around or with someone else, so you don't constantly feel the need to be doing whatever else seems more important. Something might feel important, and pull at the back of your brain, creating a stress you don't need.

I used to try and rush our routine in the morning. I would stress myself out and start my day off in the worst possible way. No one eats fast enough or gets dressed efficiently, and Brooklyn consistently puts her shoes on the wrong feet. Every single morning. (Sometimes we just let her go to school that way.) But the thing is, you can't rush kids. It's impossible. And getting your child to wake up, eat breakfast, get dressed, brush their teeth, put on their shoes and backpack without crying, and with efficiency, can only be done with practiced magic.

I had to step back and ask myself what was really driving me to be so hurried. What was more important than getting my kids ready in the morning? My work emails? A report that was due in three days that I wanted to finish early? In the morning I am with my children, and work is not my priority. It has taken time to retrain my brain. Although my job feels like it requires 24/7 attention, I can prevent my job from consuming me. And I should not let my job consume me, because that is not healthy. Once I let go of that 'need' to get the kids out the door so I could do that report that is not urgently due, I felt immense relief. Of course, mornings were still a struggle at times because we had a toddler, and then a baby on top of that, but they were much less stressful.

When you let go of the expectations and the things you think you'd rather be doing, or think you need to be doing, you can start allowing yourself to be present for your children. It takes practice. Breaking our phone habits, breaking our complaining habits, snapping out of that 'but I'm so jealous I can't do this' attitude. Being present is not always easy, but it is worth it. It is also important. Your children will pick up on your habits. They'll begin to learn what you portray to them as your values.

Being present also does not have to be perfect. There will be days we are less present than others. We're human, so that is allowed. All you can do is try to be there in the best way you are able in that moment.

Your new family priorities are what make life great. I know you know this because you decided you wanted to have children. But even then, we all need reminding from time to time. We can acknowledge the challenges of parenting and love it at the same time. It's what creates this beautifully messy, conflicted love that consumes us.

And consume you, it will. I don't think it's a bad thing, either. It is part of what makes motherhood so incredible. The guilt and frustration we might feel are only a result of the overwhelming love we feel for our children. We want the absolute best for them, and inevitably we will be hard on ourselves for that.

There are plenty of unsurprising ways that motherhood will impact your life. By now, you should know that you always expect the unexpected. Motherhood may cause you to think about your future in unexpected ways. Children have a way of making us realize what is truly important. They help us find happiness. They might help us discover our passions. They'll teach you more about who you are.

And they might change the direction for your future, or your career.

There are many women who wish to be a stay-at-home mom. This line of work was something I never felt would appeal to me. Raising kids is hard. Put that on top of basically never escaping your children and having minimal adult interaction—hard pass. At least, that's what I thought before having kids.

While I have chosen to stay in the workforce, we seriously contemplated this. Still do at times. And honestly, I am happy where I am at. I'm not looking to become a CEO. I'm not looking for a fancy management position. I like to go to work and then come home to my family. I often look at my career and realize how minuscule it is in the grand scheme of life. Nothing I am doing at my job really matters. But raising my kids? Enjoying them as a child, because they won't be small forever? That shit matters.

Seeing my kids for only an hour or two out of every day feels awful.

I enjoy my job most of the time, but it is stressful. It can be way too stressful sometimes, with other people pushing their agendas into my life, which will often bleed past normal work hours. Having to dedicate my day to a stressful workplace, and then come home to crying children is draining.

But you know what else is stressful? Planning your day around naps, potty training, teaching your kids life skills and listening to a crying child all day long, instead of that last hour of their day. You'll have never imagined that you could love someone so much that can simultaneously frustrate you so badly.

Of course, this is largely a financial discussion for many families and is a determining factor in why we decided not to try. But on the flipside, I also couldn't decide if I could handle the stress of being with my children full time. I wanted to, but I wasn't sure if it was really the right move for me. Being a stay-at-home mom would be hard. Really hard.

Each path comes with its own benefits, and they have their own challenges as well. And no matter what you choose to do, know that whatever route you take is an admirable one.

As your children will teach you more about who you are, you might be surprised about the things you discover. And how you might change your mind.

I mean...I never thought I wanted kids...and here I am writing about parenting.

I never thought I liked being by myself. And now I crave time to myself and have discovered that I am really more introverted than I realized.

I am slowing down and trying to live more in the moment, which is something I never did before. I am trying to navigate and soak up every moment of this happily hectic life I've managed to create. There is beauty in the chaos if you let yourself see it.

10 YOU MIGHT DO IT ALL OVER AGAIN

Yea, I said it.

You might do it all over again and decide to have another baby. You'll magically forget what morning sickness actually feels like. You'll forget that you lost sleep for over half of your pregnancy. (How? How do you forget what that is like? I don't know, but it happens.)

Did you really have many aches and pains?

It couldn't have been that bad, right?

You'll seem to have lost your mind, and think, "It should be easier the second time around because your body already knows what to do. Right?!"

Spoiler alert! No. No, it is not easier.

They say you forget what it's like to be pregnant, and as much as I hate to admit it (Oh, how I hate to admit this), it's true. That's why we do it again. Our subconscious is the thing that wants that second child and plays tricks on us until we agree to do it.

In the heat of my last pregnancy (literally in the heat, I did more than my fair share of complaining during the hottest Texas summer we had in almost 10 years, often referring to myself as a beached whale on the shores of hell), I swore that I'd never forget how awful it was. I mean, I won't forget now because I wrote this book while it was all fresh in my mind, but I did forget some of it after my first pregnancy. I did not forget the symptoms, but I did forget the severity of them. You know how you get a cold, and you temporarily forget what it feels like to actually breathe out of your nose? And you mourn your sense of smell for a little while? That's kind of what it's like, but in reverse. And unfortunately, after our second time around, I was quickly reminded of what pregnancy is really like within one week of peeing on that stick.

The second pregnancy is arguably harder for every woman because the biggest luxury you have in your first pregnancy is gone.

That luxury is time. You no longer have an abundance of time to take a nap, sleep in, get a pedicure, or go shopping for shoes and purses because shopping for clothes would be a cruel joke. There is no time to eat a meal by yourself. There is no time to just sit on the couch in silence and put your feet up for 15 minutes. Most of your free time is spent entertaining or caring for your first-born. My second pregnancy had less nausea, but it had many more aches and pains and much more fatigue. I could hardly blame that on the child in the womb. It was all a result of having a toddler, waddling around after her while carrying 30 extra pounds. We conveniently moved in the middle of my pregnancy, to a home that had stairs, which I could barely walk up without becoming breathless.

Life with two children is a different book altogether. It's your current chaos times two. It can mean diapers times two if your oldest isn't yet potty trained. You'll have nights where neither of your children is sleeping. We got a full dose of pandemonium as parents of two the first week I went back to work after Charlotte. Brooklyn got the flu. Charlotte was only 7 weeks old and not yet sleeping through the night, so we were up from midnight until 6 am with one of our two children at all times. It was the definition of misery...trying to keep the children quarantined, more tired than ever...and then eventually catching the flu ourselves.

Most importantly, getting a babysitter after you have two children gets a lot more expensive. (Priorities.)

But watching your oldest child interact and play with your youngest will make your heart melt.

Having a guaranteed playmate is also a good reason to have a second kid.

Oh, poor second child. The brunt of all my jokes.

But if I'm being honest, there were many times during my second pregnancy that I questioned how it would be possible to parent two children equally. How would it be possible to love two children equally? I remember thinking there was no way I could love this second baby as much as I loved Brooklyn. Surely Brooklyn would be my favorite child forever and ever and Charlotte would just have to have a stronger bond with her dad. It didn't make sense to me how I could do it.

But, somehow, the moment you meet that second baby, your heart just expands and fills with more love than you thought was humanly possible. And then you're a mom of two and it's totally weird for a while. The first time you say you have two children out loud; you will wonder how in the hell it happened. And you remember it was your subconscious that tricked you, and you'll vow to never do it again, even though you might.

I still, after asking my husband three times to go get a vasectomy—and even agreeing to this asinine idea that he could go to Vegas to get a 'vasectomy special' during March Madness so he can sit and watch basketball all day, basically on vacation—I've contemplated what it'd be like to have a third child. But then I force myself to remember that I hate pregnancy, I don't want to have sleepless nights again, and I've already given away all our baby stuff anyway, so it really doesn't make sense for us.

That trickery can get you.

But I certainly won't pressure you into a second child, because it might not be for you. If you're reading this book, then chances are you're just getting your feet wet in this raising a human being thing. I certainly wasn't sure how many kids we'd have when we first got pregnant. I was miserable and could not commit to having another child because I could not imagine doing it all over again. Having two children was a compromise between us, as Kyle really wanted three. I finally agreed to our second because I didn't want to be the one entertaining Brooklyn for the rest of her childhood. Enter the 'guaranteed playmate' joke, that also isn't really a joke at all.

And remember how I was scared to have a girl? I know that Kyle would have loved a boy (although I know he wouldn't change a thing about our lives), but I did secretly want another girl. I have two sisters and they're awesome and also my best friends. The things you think you want before you have children are almost always guaranteed to change.

Not only will I not pressure you into having a second child, but I won't even ask you if you want one. Almost immediately after Brooklyn was born, an unacceptable number of people asked us when we'd be having our second child.

Um. Excuse me?! "Slow your roll, Tina—I have not fully committed to re-living this pregnancy/newborn nightmare again. I was having contractions 24 hours ago." Don't even get me started on the people who asked if we'd try for a boy, just days after Charlotte was born. Talk to the hand, because that shit ain't happening.

I've vowed to not ask any woman this, unless I know them well enough because it can be an uncomfortable question.

In all realness, though, Kyle and I agreed that our family felt complete the minute Charlotte was placed on my chest after birth. There are some things in life you just know, and we both knew that from here on out Kyle's life would be filled with more estrogen than he might be able to handle at times, but there is nothing we would ever dream about changing.

I once heard someone say that it is the obstacles in life that bring us enjoyment. If we were to receive everything, we wanted in life without lifting a finger, would we actually enjoy it? With that in the back of my mind, the misery I experienced during pregnancy was obviously a necessity. Would we cherish a baby's giggle as much if we didn't ever hear her cry? There is no pleasure in having something if it didn't take work to get it. It's the truth about anything in life and especially about having children.

As hard as it is, we do it because we love them. Because your tiny little love terrorist will have your heartstrings wrapped around her tiny fingers.

Or maybe, less wrapped, and more of a death grip, like when they pull your hair and won't let go.

And as hard as parenting is, you'll remember it doesn't last forever. Your baby will grow. You'll have a phase where she'll learn to walk and run around, and you get no baby cuddles. The squishiness starts to fade. You have a toddler, not a baby. And that is when you'll get tricked.

You'll forget what it's like to get up in the middle of the night with a baby.

Did you know there are some women who don't mind getting up in the middle of the night to feed a baby? In fact, I have heard one woman say she 'loves it.' While it's baffling to me, that could be you! And I can understand why some women might feel that way. It's been established long ago that I am not an overly emotional person. Although I was never into breastfeeding, that is a bond that many women love to experience with their babies. The dark and quiet in the middle of the night where only you and your child get such an intimate experience together. (That is, if you aren't staring at your iPhone.)

I did find that one of the cutest moments I'd have with my babies came after their raging cries of hunger in the middle of the night. They're angry, and I'd hurriedly try to maneuver them out of their swaddle or sleepsuit, changing a diaper as fast as possible. They're kicking their legs and flailing their arms, and then they get the boob or the bottle, and it is the ultimate relief.

I'd see the immediate calm. Even if it was because of an end to their hunger, and not necessarily being held by me, it still brought a feeling of calm over me, too.

And, many times, I'd experience the sleepy cuddles and milk-drunk smiles on their faces when they're content and ready to fall back asleep. Those are the moments that trick your brain into forgetting the bad stuff. Because, although I joke about how awful all the bad stuff is, without the bad stuff, we really wouldn't appreciate all the good stuff. And those sleepy cuddles and milk-drunk smiles are pretty damn good.

But that is the power these little babes have over us. These little love terrorists. Newborn warfare is filled with unequal weapons of mass heart-melting destruction, to which you have no protection.

Their secret weapons are in the form of baby snuggles and giggles. First steps or first words. Reciting the alphabet or surprising you with a song they just learned. Hugs and kisses, and when they say 'I love you, Mommy' before bed.

Have kids, they said.

Your heart will melt, they said.

And they were right.

ABOUT THE AUTHOR

Alysia Lowe Ehle finished her PhD in Chemistry, only to leave the field of science in pursuit of more creative endeavors. Landing herself in marketing and agency life, she's found value in the written word.

Striving to help others improve their lives, she writes about a number of topics including parenting, minimalism, and environmentalism. She approaches all topics with a realistic attitude, as demonstrated in the book, *Have Kids, They Said.* When approaching a problem or topic with candor and relatability, problems become easier to solve.

Born in 1986 in Waupaca, Wisconsin, Alysia currently lives in Dallas, Texas with her husband and two daughters. Read more about her life and work at TheArtsyMinimalist.com.